A MISCELLANY OF OBJECTS FROM

# SIR JOHN SOANE'S MUSEUM

A MISCELLANY OF OBJECTS FROM

# SIR JOHN SOANE'S MUSEUM

CONSISTING OF PAINTINGS, ARCHITECTURAL DRAWINGS AND OTHER
CURIOSITIES FROM THE COLLECTION OF
SIR JOHN SOANE

PETER THORNTON
AND HELEN DOREY

PHOTOGRAPHS BY OLE WOLDBYE

LAURENCE KING

Published 1992 by Laurence King Publishing

British Library Cataloguing in Publication Data

Thornton, Peter
Sir John Soane's Museum.
I. Title II. Dorey, Helen
720

ISBN 1-85669-015-6
ISBN 1-85669-029-6 pbk

Designed by Karen Stafford, DQP, London
Typeset by Tek Art Ltd, Croydon, England
Printed and bound in Singapore by Star Standard Industries PTE

*Frontispiece:* View of the Dome Area with a bust of John Soane
by Sir Francis Chantrey, 1829.

# CONTENTS

# PREFACE

Soon after being appointed Curator in 1984 I began to recognise that there was a need for some kind of picture-book to supplement the Museum's excellent and extremely informative guide-book, the so-called *New Description*. It was important not to clash with the market for which the *New Description* was written, and eventually I decided to produce a picture-book that concentrated, not on the building (which has been the subject of numerous publications, several of them of great merit), but on some of the objects that are to be found in the collections formed by Sir John Soane.

The selection I made, now some four years ago, was a very personal one, consisting of items that gave me pleasure or that seemed interesting to me for one reason or another. My intention was to draw attention to the wide range of objects in this curious building and, in doing so, to throw light on various aspects of Soane's character, aspirations and career. So this is a book about objects; it is not a life of Soane, nor is it a description of his house – although it touches upon both these subjects at many points. In a sense, the seemingly random scatter of information that is introduced in the long captions devoted to each of the objects illustrated here echoes the apparently haphazard arrangement of Soane's collections which, however, was undoubtedly calculated to produce an impression that had significance for him and that, he hoped, would be understood at a deep level by those who visited his house. As he himself explained, his juxtaposing of objects was intended to inspire a reaction in his beholder that was analogous to reading poetry. It was to some extent at an unconscious level that this 'poetry of architecture', as he called it, was meant to convey its message.

It will at any rate be seen that the total effect conveyed by our pictures and these captions is one of richness – in the variety of objects, in their disposition throughout this small building, in the imagination of the man who assembled them, and in his generosity in presenting them with his house to the nation.

Helen Dorey was the Museum's Secretary when I embarked on this project. She came to us after having read history at Oxford. I asked her to help me with some of the captions and she soon demonstrated her ability in the field of historical research, to the extent that she was eventually appointed to a curatorial post and was invited by me to become co-author of this book. She wrote the short essay, to be found after the picture section, on Soane as a collector, which contains information that has not been published before.

We would like to thank our colleagues on the Museum's staff for their constant help in many ways and we are also much indebted to many people for information that is incorporated in our captions, most notably Leslie Harris, Ruth Tschäpe, Ann Jenner, Geoffrey Godden, Graham Collard, Valentin Kochel, Geneviève Cuisset, Malcolm Baker, John Mallet, Anthony Radcliffe, Gertrude Seideman and Robert J. Reichner.

All the photographs in this book were taken by Ole Woldbye who is on the staff of the Museum of Decorative Arts in Copenhagen. He came over specifically to carry out this exercise. As I was already familiar with his work, I was not surprised to see that the result of his stay was a series of photographs which bring out in an admirable way the character of each of the objects that I selected. A substantial contribution towards the cost of this photography was made by Mr. Anthony Dorey.

Lincoln's Inn Fields
October 1991

Peter Thornton
Curator

# INTRODUCTION

Sir John Soane (1753–1837) was born the son of a bricklayer near Reading in Berkshire and rose to become one of England's greatest architects. His architectural career began when he entered the office of George Dance the Younger, at the age of fifteen. In about 1770 he transferred to the office of Henry Holland. During the 1770s the young Soane began to make a name for himself. Having enrolled at the Royal Academy as a student in 1771, aged eighteen, he began to enter his drawings for Royal Academy competitions, winning the silver medal in 1772 and the gold medal (at the second attempt) in 1776. Following this triumph, the architect Sir William Chambers introduced Soane to King George III, who awarded him a travelling scholarship to Italy for three years. Soane set off in March 1778, travelling to Rome via France. During the next year and a half he visited Naples, Paestum, Calabria, Sicily, Malta, Venice, Verona, Vicenza, Mantua and Parma – constantly measuring, sketching and recording his impressions of the finest antique and renaissance buildings. He also made contact with many of those of the nobility and gentry who later helped him in his career. In 1780 Soane cut short his stay in Italy after 'repeated solicitations' from the mercurial Frederick Hervey, Earl-Bishop of Derry in Ireland and returned to England via Switzerland, Germany and Holland, ready to undertake work for the Bishop at Downhill in Ireland. It rapidly became clear that no commission was going to materialise and Soane was thrown back on his own resources.

It was at this point that Soane commenced his own practice in London, in 1781, initially designing mainly small country houses in East Anglia and the Home Counties (see Fig. 30). In 1788 he was appointed Architect to the Bank of England, a post he held until his retirement at the age of eighty in 1833. In his forty-five years at the Bank Soane rebuilt Sir Robert Taylor's earlier Bank buildings and constructed a greatly enlarged new Bank which was acclaimed as a masterpiece by his own as well as later generations. Among Soane's other appointments during his long career were those of Architect Attached to the Office of Works (responsible for buildings in Whitehall and Westminster), Clerk of Works to the Royal Hospital, Chelsea, and Grand Superintendent of Works for the Freemasons. In 1831 he was knighted by William IV, and in 1835 he was awarded a special gold medal by The Architects of England in recognition of his achievements.

Not least among these were his House, Museum and Library at 13 Lincoln's Inn Fields, which he bequeathed to the nation by a private Act of Parliament in 1833, for the benefit of 'Amateurs and Students of Painting, Sculpture and Architecture'.

Soane's connection with Lincoln's Inn Fields had begun in 1792 with the purchase of No. 12, which he demolished and rebuilt with an office at the back of the main house, on the site previously occupied by the stables. He was able to buy the house because of the inheritance which had come to him through his wife's uncle, the wealthy builder George Wyatt, who died in 1790. His death provided Soane and his wife with a large secure income independent of his business. It was this which enabled Soane to build up his remarkable collection. Soane may well have selected Lincoln's Inn Fields for its proximity to the Royal Academy, which moved into Somerset House, on the Strand, designed by Sir William Chambers, in 1780. By the time Joseph Gandy painted his watercolour view of the Soane family in the Breakfast Parlour at No. 12 in November 1798 (Fig. 94) Soane already had an extensive Library – at least six bookcases-full – which he had devoted several days to cataloguing in 1793, a year when his total expenditure on books is recorded as £338.14s.2d. He purchased plaster casts worth £40.10s.0d. at the sale of the effects of the Scottish architect James Playfair in 1795, had them mounted in wooden frames and set them up in a passage running between the front part of No. 12 and the office at the back, and used solely for the display of 'plaisters'.

In 1800 Soane purchased Pitzhanger Manor, Ealing, which he then rebuilt (1800–02) as his country villa (see Fig. 41). He always said that he had done this to foster 'a taste for the fine arts' in his elder son, John, whom, he hoped, would follow him into the architectural profession. It was after his acquisition of Pitzhanger that Soane began to earn a reputation as a collector. He bought the Cawdor Vase at Christie's in 1800 and placed it prominently in the front parlour at Pitzhanger. Extensive purchases of antique cinerary urns, vases and marbles followed in the next year, from the sales of the collections of the Earl of Bessborough and the Duke of St Albans. In February 1802, Mrs. Soane bid at Christie's for Hogarth's *Rake's Progress* acquiring the eight canvases for £570. Mrs. Soane also purchased two watercolours by J.M.W. Turner from Turner's Gallery in 1804 (see Fig. 37). In 1805 Soane purchased ten Clérisseau drawings from Dr. Thomas Monro for 100 guineas and two paintings from Boydell's Shakespeare Gallery. All these purchases were destined for Pitzhanger.

In 1806 Soane was appointed Professor of Architecture at the Royal Academy. This entailed giving a series of six public lectures annually. He immediately embarked on a wide-ranging and intensive study of all aspects of architecture in preparation. The immense scope of his researches is demonstrated by the fact that his first lecture was not delivered until 1809. This public teaching role must have been a great stimulus to Soane as a collector and certainly from this point on he saw a public role for his collection. His Royal Academy students were able to come to his house at Lincoln's Inn Fields the day before and the day after each lecture to examine the illustrations (see Fig. 32) and, presumably, to inspect models and casts as well. In addition, the wide range of his reading in preparation for the lectures may have encouraged Soane to purchase items such as a 'capital of Hindoo architecture', and, later, to acquire term figures from Furnival's Inn, nearby on High Holborn, when it was demolished. Soane was not personally involved in this work but acquired the pieces because they were good examples of the 17th-century style. By this time he was also training pupils in his office and they, like his Royal Academy students, benefitted from his collection.

It seems that from 1807 onwards Pitzhanger Manor became an increasing burden. With Soane's appointment to the Royal Hospital at Chelsea in that year came a house there, and the running of three establishments seems rapidly to have become too much for Mrs. Soane. Pitzhanger was too far out of London to benefit Soane's Royal Academy students and Soane was becoming increasingly disillusioned by the lack of interest in architecture shown by his own two sons. It is perhaps significant that when he purchased his marvellous large Canaletto 'Venetian Scene' (Fig. 83) in 1807 it was hung, not at Pitzhanger, but at Chelsea. In the summer of 1808 Soane bought the freehold of No. 13, Lincoln's Inn Fields (now the Soane Museum) and, while leaving the sitting tenant, George Booth Tyndale, in the front part of the house, set about preparing an extension of his offices across the back premises. The designs made provision for a 'plaister room' or 'model room' which evolved into the present Dome area. The Dome and new offices were completed in 1809 and in November of that year Pitzhanger Manor was put on the market. It was sold in 1810 and the contents moved to Lincoln's Inn Fields, where early watercolours show many of them piled into the new Dome. In 1810 and 1811 Lincoln's Inn Fields must have been impossibly crowded, despite the new extension, but Soane still could not resist accepting the gift of the large cast of the Apollo Belvedere (see Fig. 74), which had once belonged to Lord Burlington, from the architect John White.

In 1812 Soane negotiated with Mr. Tyndale, the long-suffering tenant of No. 13, to take over the front part of No. 13 which he then demolished and rebuilt, making the Dome area and his old office at the back of No. 12 accessible from No. 13. The Soanes moved into No. 13 in 1813.

Soane spent the next quarter of a century adding to his collections and continually altering, re-arranging and perfecting No. 13. Seemingly undeterred by Mrs. Soane's early death in 1815 at the age of fifty-one, he continued to expand and alter the house, often as a direct result of acquisitions. In 1816 the Study and Dressing-Room were remodelled to take the collection of antique marbles collected in Rome in the 1790s by Charles Heathcote Tatham for Henry Holland (see Fig. 16), Soane's former master. The acquisition of a large number of marbles, terracottas and casts from Robert Adam's sale in 1818 led to the re-designing of the lower office at the back of the house to create the Colonnade, giving additional exhibition space. On acquiring No. 14 in 1824, aged seventy-one, Soane, for the third time in Lincoln's Inn Fields, demolished and completely rebuilt, constructing his Picture Room on the site of the stables, with the Monk's Parlour below it, and also retaining the courtyard, in which he created the Monk's Yard, with its mock ruins, the Monk's Well and the Monk's Tomb.

Soane had purchased Hogarth's *An Election* series in 1823, at the sale of the effects of Mrs. Garrick (widow of the celebrated Shakespearian actor David Garrick, who had purchased them from Hogarth himself). The need to provide an appropriate setting for this splendid acquisition must have spurred Soane to the purchase of No. 14 and the creation of the Picture Room. Although after the re-building of No. 14 and the adding of an extra storey to No. 13 the following year, Soane did little major structural work, he did continue to make minor alterations to accommodate the growing number of perspective views of his own works and framed engravings which he wished to display. In particular, in the late 1820s he added hinged 'movable planes' to the walls of the North Drawing-Room and the Breakfast Room. Soane's last alterations were carried out in 1834 when, aged eighty-one, he expanded the space available on the first floor by incorporating the former open verandah at the front of the house into the South Drawing-Room. In the same year he altered the hanging arches between the Dining-Room and the Library and installed Henry Howard's ceiling paintings.

Soane's Hogarths and his collection of Adam drawings are fairly widely known. What is less often appreciated is the exceptional diversity and scope of the contents of his two houses in Lincoln's Inn Fields. The total number of inventoried objects is about three thousand and includes Greek, Roman and Egyptian antiquities, casts, bronzes, gems, jewellery, medals, silver, furniture, clocks, barometers, natural objects and curiosities, arms, Peruvian pottery, Chinese ceramics, medieval tiles and pottery, sculpture, a mummy's head, mummified cats and a rat. In addition there are the oil paintings, watercolours, 30,000 architectural drawings, approximately 150 models, nearly 8,000 books and Soane's personal Archive.

Soane prepared his Museum personally, spending huge sums of money and gathering items for their intrinsic value, their appearance or their associations. It was intended as a living demonstration of his belief that 'Architecture is the Queen of the Fine Arts . . . Painting and Sculpture are her handmaids, assisted by whom . . . she combines and displays all the mighty powers of Music, Poetry and Allegory'. Hence the fact that when Soane's old friend John Britton published the first account of the Museum in 1827, its title was *The Union of Architecture, Sculpture and Painting*. Soane wished to ennoble architecture at a time when it was not considered as important among the arts as painting and sculpture. He wished to create a poetic setting, using architecture as an expressive art form evoking emotions and associations of antiquity. For this reason he eschewed didactic arrangements by periods and different cultures of the sort created in the celebrated contemporary French displays of Cassas and Lenoir. Instead he displayed his collections mingled together. The museum was to be not just a repository but an inspirational setting; a springboard for the imagination.

Soane published three *Descriptions* of his residence, in 1830, 1832 and 1835, with the aim of giving 'some idea of the manner in which the Works of Art are arranged and the different effects are produced . . . [so as to leave] as little as possible to the chance of their being removed from the positions relatively assigned to them; they having been arranged as studies for my own mind, and being intended similarly to benefit the Artists of future generations'. In the Soane Museum Act of Parliament, passed in 1833, he stipulated that the arrangements should be kept in the state in which they were left at his death. Thus we have in places still preserved an authentic record in his arrangements of how Soane's imagination worked.

In the late 18th and the early 19th centuries it was not unusual for an architect to have a collection of architectural specimens, both original antique marbles and casts. Robert Adam, James Playfair, Willey Reveley and Henry Holland had such collections and Soane acquired items from all four. Architectural students copied fragments as art students copied paintings and those who were unable to go on a Grand Tour of their own were thus enabled to see elements of antique architecture and ornament in three dimensions. Soane wrote in Royal Academy Lecture 6, 'It is of the most serious import to the Artist to be able to trace every species of decoration to its source and likewise to be well acquainted with the different styles of executing ornaments to be found in the Ancient World. This knowledge will be most effectively attained by . . . studying the Taste, Character and Expression of the original works on the spot. As some of the young architects cannot have this advantage, Casts in Plaister, carefully made from them must . . . supply that deficiency'.

Soane's was the collection of a working architect and was used as an anthology of antique architecture and decoration as well as a teaching collection. He described the Upper Drawing Office, where his pupils worked, as 'peculiarly adapted for study . . . surrounded with marble Fragments and Casts, from the remains of antiquity and from the Artists of the cinquecento; and the drawers are filled with architectural drawings and prints, for the instructions of the pupils'. He hoped that after his death architects of future generations would use his collection for reference in the same way. He firmly believed that it was impossible to achieve 'perfection in architecture' without a visual training in all the arts. His collection of antiquities is therefore not merely architectural; it ranges far more widely, as this book of pictures is intended to demonstrate.

# PLAN OF THE GROUND FLOORS OF NOs. 12, 13 & 14 LINCOLN'S INN FIELDS AS EXISTING

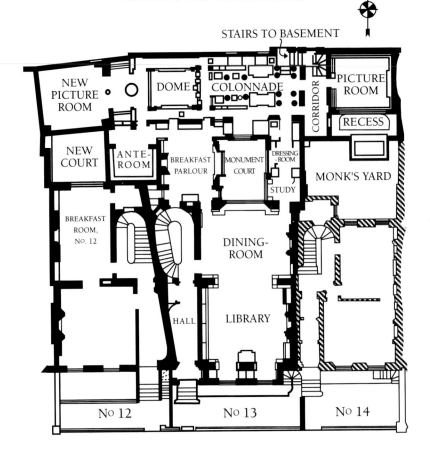

STAIRS TO BASEMENT

NEW PICTURE ROOM

DOME

COLONNADE

CORRIDOR

PICTURE ROOM

RECESS

NEW COURT

ANTE-ROOM

BREAKFAST PARLOUR

MONUMENT COURT

DRESSING-ROOM

STUDY

MONK'S YARD

BREAKFAST ROOM, No. 12

DINING-ROOM

HALL

LIBRARY

No 12    No 13    No 14

## PLAN OF THE BASEMENT AS EXISTING

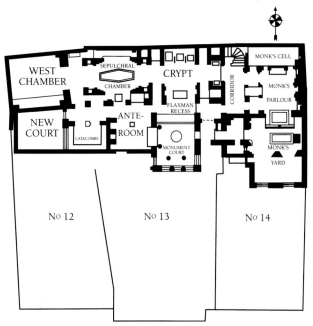

WEST CHAMBER

SEPULCHRAL CHAMBER

CRYPT

CORRIDOR

MONK'S CELL

MONK'S PARLOUR

FLAXMAN RECESS

NEW COURT

CATACOMBS

ANTE-ROOM

MONUMENT COURT

MONK'S YARD

No 12    No 13    No 14

## PLAN OF THE FIRST FLOOR AS EXISTING

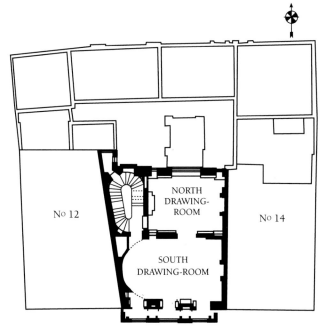

No 12

NORTH DRAWING-ROOM

No 14

SOUTH DRAWING-ROOM

# THE FRONT HALL

**Fig. 1** View of the Front Hall of No. 13 Lincoln's Inn Fields in 1825. Sir John Soane had an album made entitled *Sketches and Drawings of the Museum of J. Soane Esq., RA*, probably in 1825, at which date he had not been knighted. The watercolours were executed by members of his drawing-office staff, primarily by C.J. Richardson and J.M. Gandy. A few watercolours of the 1830s were included by Soane later, the album coming to contain about 125 views of the house (mainly interiors) and some of the objects in the collection. It forms an astonishingly informative record of how the house appeared in Soane's day.

The Entrance Hall has not changed greatly. When this view was made the solid wood front door was on the outer plane of what is today an open porch. The stained glass visible here is in an inner door in the position now occupied by the front door. When Soane later moved the front door back to create the porch the stained glass was put in a new fanlight and inner door under the arch in the foreground of this view. In 1908 new swing doors were fitted incorporating Soane's stained glass and these are the doors to be seen in the inner hall today. Originally, the floors were of pine boards, scrubbed white. Linoleum, laid in much more recent times, is an example of that institutionalisation which so easily takes over a historic house that is open to the public: it has a dark effect quite unlike the snow-like appearance of the original scheme. The simulated porphyry walls would also have been a much lighter colour than they are today.

**Sketches and Drawings Volume (Vol. 82), p.4**

**222mm × 130mm**

# THE LIBRARY AND DINING-ROOM

**Fig 2**    A watercolour view made in 1825 showing the Dining-Room end of this dual-purpose room, seen from the Library end. When many guests came to dinner, Soane could have the dining table extended into the Library. Soane was always making changes to his rooms, right up to the time of his death in 1837. After this scene was painted he installed a fine portrait of himself by Sir Thomas Lawrence over the fireplace, replaced the ornaments on the chimneypiece (which include Fig. 105 and its pair) with a model of the Board of Trade offices he designed at the entrance to Downing Street on Whitehall, had scenes from the story of Pandora painted on the ceiling by Henry Howard, RA and altered the shape of the arcading of the screen-like division between the two parts of the room. In this watercolour a glimpse of the architectural Pasticcio (see Fig. 24) can be seen through the window looking on to the Monument Court. Note the stained glass across the bottom of the window. This survives, although it was damaged in the Second World War. The two large panels at either end, showing 'The Creation' and 'The Last Judgement' (both Swiss *c.*1600) have recently been replaced in their original positions as shown here, and the other three will be replaced once they have been repaired.
**Sketches and Drawings Volume (Vol. 82), p.8**
**180mm × 284mm**

**Fig. 3**  A watercolour dated 2nd October 1825 showing in detail the objects then arranged on the west pier of the screen dividing the Dining-Room and Library, the whole of which may be seen in Fig. 2.

Topping the pyramidal arrangement is a model of the Soane Monument, enclosed in a brass-framed glass case, which still stands in the same position today. This painted wood model must have been made in 1816, soon after the death of Soane's wife, Elizabeth, in November the previous year. On the dome is an inscription that reads, 'Chère amie je ne peux plus entendre ta voix – apprends moi ce que je dois faire – pour remplir tes souhaits'. Soane's eldest son John was buried in the

same tomb, which still stands in the burial ground of St-Giles-in-the-Fields (now St Pancras Gardens, close to St Pancras Station), on his death in 1823, and Sir John Soane himself was buried there on 30th January 1837, ten days after his death. The lineaments of the finished tomb follow the model closely. The form is characteristic of Soane's architecture at the height of his career and incorporates a version of his favourite shallow dome which here forms a canopy over an upright sarcophagus of white marble.

Around the model in this watercolour are arranged twelve smaller objects, all very recent purchases in October 1825 when it was made. They had all been bought at the Charles Yarnold sale on 11th June 1825. They seem to have been specially arranged in these positions for this watercolour as they are not shown in other views of the room made in that year. To the left of the model is a bronze lamp (Museum Number S114) with an early Christian monogram, which dates, if authentic, from the late 4th or 5th centuries BC. It had been illustrated in Montfaucon's *L'Antiquité Expliquée*, 1719, so must have been regarded as rather special by Soane. It cost £6 10s. The central Egyptian bronze figure below the model (Museum Number S126) is of unknown date but appeared in the Yarnold sale catalogue as a separate lot described as the 'Elephant-headed Isis'. Around it are other small terracottas and bronzes which all formed one lot in the sale and were described as 'seven . . . brought by Mr Belzoni from Thebes' (see also Fig. 55). In front is a 15th- or early 16th-century brass chrismatory which cost Soane 17 shillings. This piece of English church plate was described in the sale catalogue as 'a large ancient pix box to contain the Holy wafers, with inscription'. It is now on display in the Monk's Parlour. Top right is 'An antique Roman vase found at Cologne, in Germany, very curious'. This can still be seen in the Library. Also shown are items described in the Yarnold sale catalogue as 'two glass lachrymotories' (glass phials usually found in Roman tombs and thought by early archaeologists to have been vases for tears). These items do not appear in the 1837 Inventory of the Museum's contents and are no longer in the collection. They were presumably broken or given away during Soane's own lifetime.

**Sketches and Drawings Volume (Vol. 82), p.10**
**318mm × 200mm**

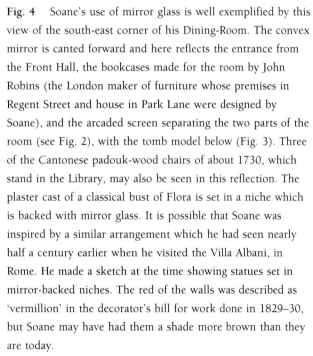

Fig. 4    Soane's use of mirror glass is well exemplified by this view of the south-east corner of his Dining-Room. The convex mirror is canted forward and here reflects the entrance from the Front Hall, the bookcases made for the room by John Robins (the London maker of furniture whose premises in Regent Street and house in Park Lane were designed by Soane), and the arcaded screen separating the two parts of the room (see Fig. 2), with the tomb model below (Fig. 3). Three of the Cantonese padouk-wood chairs of about 1730, which stand in the Library, may also be seen in this reflection. The plaster cast of a classical bust of Flora is set in a niche which is backed with mirror glass. It is possible that Soane was inspired by a similar arrangement which he had seen nearly half a century earlier when he visited the Villa Albani, in Rome. He made a sketch at the time showing statues set in mirror-backed niches. The red of the walls was described as 'vermillion' in the decorator's bill for work done in 1829–30, but Soane may have had them a shade more brown than they are today.

During his two-year stay in Italy he visited Pompeii and brought back a fragment of plaster painted a reddish brown (Museum Number L130), which could well be what he had in mind when he adopted a Pompeian scheme for this room. He may also have been influenced by Angelo Campanella's coloured engravings of frescoed Roman walls excavated at the Villa Negroni in Rome, some of which may be seen in the Breakfast Parlour (see Fig. 96).

Fig. 5    Astronomical clock by Raingo of Paris; about 1800. It has been suggested that the original model for this type of clock was designed by Napoleon's favoured architect, Charles Percier, either for the Tuileries Palace or for Malmaison (see Fig. 11). It is thought that after the Peace of Amiens in 1802 the French clock-maker came over to London and sold six of these clocks to the Prince Regent (later George IV) for himself and his five brothers. The present clock belonged to Frederick, Duke of York, who died in 1827, whereupon Soane acquired it for £75 and placed it in his Dining-Room where it has stood ever since. The case is of amboyna wood with ormolu mounts and the clock mechanism is attached to an orrery, which can also work independently. This combination of mechanisms means that the clock shows not only the time but also the day of the week, the day of the month and the month of the year, as well as the appropriate sign of the zodiac, the rotation of the earth upon its axis, the movement of the earth round the sun, the movement of the moon round the earth and the phases of the moon. In addition a revolving dial above the globe enables one to see the time and hour of the day or night in any given part of the world. If the orrery is operated separately it can be speeded up so that a 'practical illustration of the elements of cosmography and geography' is given. Five clocks of this type are recorded as surviving in recent times. One illustrated in that fashion-journal, Ackermann's *Repository*, issue III, May 1824, is described as 'forming a very useful and tasteful ornament for the drawing-room or library'.
**Museum number: L66    H: 68cm, Base dia: 38.9cm**

**Fig. 6**   This Greek vase was formerly among those placed by Soane on brackets and shelves in his Library. It is a bell *krater* of the type produced in one of the Greek colonies in southern Italy (Campania) and dates from the 4th century BC. It was bought for Soane by James Adams of Portsmouth at the sale of the effects of the Reverend Charles North at Rectory House, Alverstoke, Hampshire, on 12th October 1825, in which it was part of lot 23 described as 'A small Campana vase with the Head of a Faun contrasted with a Head of Proserpine'. Dr. Cambitoglou has attributed the decoration of this vase to the painter of another bell *krater* in Oxford and has tentatively suggested naming this artist 'the Soane painter'. Although one cannot claim that this vessel is one of the great creations of ceramic art, several of Soane's other 'Grecian urns' are of good quality and the so-called Cawdor Vase, which stands on the pier table in this room, is distinguished on account of its size and decoration.

**Museum number: L6 (Vermeule 543)    19cm × 16.8cm**

**Fig. 7**   Original estimate for the Axminster carpets, acquired in 1823 and still in their original positions on the floor of the Dining-Room and Library. There are three separate carpets, one for the Dining-Room, one for the Library and a small one for the narrower part of the room between the two main areas. As the document shows, two hearthrugs were also provided to lie in front of the fireplaces and there were two further pieces to go by the doors. The total cost finally came to £81. 15*s*. (there was a rebate) paid to Samuel Luck, who had a carpet-

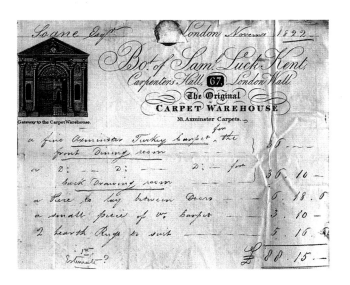

warehouse in the City, at Carpenters' Hall, a view of which is printed on the bill-head. Luck seems to have made a speciality of dealing in Axminster carpets which were the most expensive form of floor covering made in this country at the time and therefore constituted a conspicuous item of expenditure by Soane, one that would not have gone un-noticed by the discerning. Part of the Library carpet may be seen in Fig. 2.

The two sheets of mirror glass fitted into the front of the pier table at the south end of the Library provide a viewer standing by the entrance-door with a reflection of the carpet; there can be no doubt that Soane created this as a calculated effect, the subtlety of which would be lost on most visitors. This is a good example of the kind of almost conspiratorial effects in which Soane delighted; only those who allow themselves the time, and are in tune with his way of thinking, are likely to appreciate such conceits as they pass through a room. This bill is to be found among Soane's papers which form part of an extensive archive that is an amazingly rich source of information about Soane, his private and public life, his business as a leading architect and about the social and intellectual life of his times.

**Archive reference: P.C. XVI.A.4.3**

Fig. 8   A selection of decorated paper book-covers on volumes in Soane's Library dating from the late 18th and early 19th centuries. The Library contains numerous fine bindings as well as many that are merely workaday covers of leather for volumes that were to be handled frequently. Of great interest, however, are the many volumes that remain in their original paper covers, like those shown here. These have never been bound, perhaps because Soane wanted to save the expense or perhaps because he thought the decorative paper covers in themselves attractive. Two of the five papers shown here are marbled, one is a paste-paper and two are block-printed.

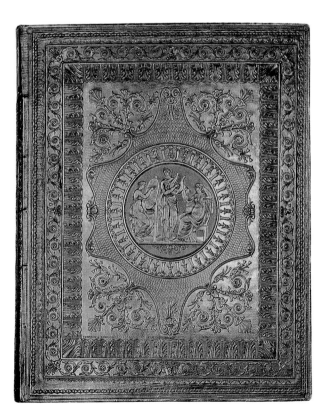

Fig. 9   Stamped bookbinding, probably about 1830, bearing the name of Remnant & Edmonds of London who introduced the method of whole-plate impression on leather bindings in 1829. Soane must have been very interested in this new technique and had the firm encase a book of 1794 which he had bought on 18th March 1815 from the bookseller Boone for 5s. 6d. – *The works of the late Professor Camper on the Connexion between the Science of Anatomy and the Arts of Drawing, Painting and Statuary, in two books. . . with a new method of sketching heads, national features and the portraits of individuals, with accuracy, etc.* . . ., translated out of the Dutch by T. Cogan, M.D., London 1794. The design of the covers, which are identical, front and back, is an elegant expression of late Regency taste. This technique was to be used widely for albums and the like, later in the 19th century.
**Architectural Library, 31.A.    29cm × 23.75cm**

**Fig. 10**  *Pages 18–19*: Hand-coloured plate by Pietro Fabris showing the uncovering of the Temple of Isis at Pompeii in June 1785. From *Campi Phlegraei* (the burning fields) by Sir William Hamilton (1730–1803), being 'Observations on the volcanos of the two Sicilies as they have been communicated to the Royal Society of London by Sir William Hamilton, KB, FRS, His Britannic Majesty's envoy extraordinary and plenipotentiary at the Court of Naples'. The first two volumes of this work were published in 1776 in Naples at Hamilton's personal expense and a third supplementary volume appeared in 1799 dealing with the eruption of Mount Vesuvius in August of that year. Soane purchased his copy of the complete work on 2nd March 1799 from the bookseller M. Faulder for £20. In October 1802 he paid Edward Lawrence in the Strand for 'half-binding Hamilton on Volcanos 1s. 6d.'

During his time as British ambassador to the Bourbon court of Naples and Sicily from 1764–1800, Sir William devoted all his spare time to collecting vases and other antiquities, taking an active part in the excavation of Pompeii and Herculaneum and, in particular, sending graphic reports about the activity of Mount Vesuvius, Mount Etna and other volcanic phenomena to the Royal Society (of which he was elected a Fellow in 1766). It is these reports, with Fabris's illustrations, that make up the three volumes of *Campi Phlegraei*. They are regarded as pioneering works in modern vulcanology and Hamilton himself was nicknamed by Horace Walpole 'the Professor of Earthquakes'. The book has texts in both English and French (the language of the court of Naples) on each page and the views show volcanic scenery, Vesuvus erupting, lava flowing through the countryside, lakes formed in extinct craters and volcanic specimens as well as the uncovering of Pompeii and Herculaneum. Many of the plates show Hamilton himself, on horseback or on foot, wearing a tricorne and a red coat, observing through a telescope, making drawings and showing Vesuvius erupting to distinguished guests (visitors included the Emperor Joseph II, the King and Queen of Sicily and James Boswell). In four years Hamilton climbed Vesuvius no less than twenty-two times and made expeditions all over southern Italy trying to determine the extent of volcanic influence on the landscape.

The plate illustrated here shows the Temple of Isis emerging from the volcanic ash and lava which had covered the city of Pompeii in the great eruption of Vesuvius in 79 AD. The uncovering of this Temple was an important milestone in the discovery of Pompeii – its decoration and furniture were found in an almost perfect state of preservation along with the carbonized remains of the priest and his last meal. Hamilton was present when the Temple of Isis was uncovered but his accompanying text for this plate shows that he was primarily interested in what was revealed about the volcanic origins of the landscape. He wrote 'the intention of this plate is to shew the exact similitude of the strata of rapilli and erupted matter that cover this City, (and whose volcanick origin cannot be disputed) to the soil of many parts of the neighbourhood of Naples'. He points out the vineyards flourishing in the good top-soil, which led to the discovery of the city by local people digging holes to plant their vines, and also the lower strata proving 'diverse eruptions of Vesuvius, long before that which destroy'd the City and which is the first recorded by History'.

Soane visited Naples and southern Italy in 1779 with his patron, Frederick Hervey, Bishop of Derry, who was particularly interested in vulcanology. The Bishop was an old friend of Hamilton and had been injured while ascending Vesuvius in his company during the eruption of 24th March 1766. Soane must have been introduced to Sir William while he was in Naples. During his visit he made at least two journeys with the bishop to look at volcanic features and on 20th January 1779 he climbed Vesuvius. He also inspected the Theatre in Herculaneum, the only part of that city which at that time could be reached and then only by crawling through underground galleries. Naturally, he visited Pompeii – three times – and despite a ban on sketching made drawings, measurements and notes. A plan and elevation of the Temple of Isis from 'sketches made by stealth by moonlight' was later produced for one of his Royal Academy lectures (see Fig. 32). When Soane left the area in March 1779 he noted that his last view was across the bay to Vesuvius.

This part of Italy obviously continued to fascinate him. He carefully preserved 'a piece of cinder from Vesuvius', still in the Museum's collection (L135) along with a chunk of red-painted stucco from Pompeii (see Fig. 4). He also later purchased a large cork model showing Pompeii in 1820 and was given more fragments of moulding and pavement from the city by a Miss Swinnerton. He often recalled his visit to Italy and among the references in his *Notebook* (his diary) is the entry for the 18th March 1828 which reads '1778 Wed[nesday] morn[i]ng; set out from the Golden Cross, Ch[aring] Cross for Dover with R. Brettingham for Italy – 50 years ago'.

**Architectural Library, SDR, Pl.41**   213 × 394mm

**Fig. 11** *Opposite*: Another book of outstanding interest in Soane's library is one dedicated to Joséphine Bonaparte in 1798, before she became Empress. On the cover of the superbly bound volume is the inscription 'Madame Bonaparte', framed with gold tooling. The work is entitled *Palais, Maisons et autre édifices modernes dessinés à Rome* and was compiled by Charles Percier and P.F.L. Fontaine, the two young architects who were soon to become the preferred architects of Napoleon and his wife (see Figs. 5 and 120). This book is concerned with late 15th- and 16th-century villas and palaces in Rome as well as some buildings of a later date; it represents an important revival of interest in Renaissance architecture and was to have considerable influence on the character of French architecture and ornament of the Empire Period. The engraved plates in this publication are in the outline style favoured at this period for works on artistic matters, a style embodying no shading or other form of modelling that would produce a three-dimensional effect. In this dedication volume, however, duplicate plates are bound in, in pairs facing each other, and the architects have painted one of each pair in its true colours, complete with chiaroscuro. The result is to bring startlingly alive the otherwise rather dry outline illustrations of the standard edition (of which Soane also owned a copy).

The year after this book was given to Joséphine, Percier and Fontaine were entrusted with the task of building and decorating the villa at Malmaison for her. It was to become her favourite residence and was a building that epitomised the style for which they became famous. Soane visited Malmaison in 1819 and, as his companion William Pilkington recorded at the time, 'we were both much interested . . . [in] those things which once had the care and attention of Josephine'.

**Architectural Library, 11    420mm × 320mm**

Among the books in the Library in Soane's time was a volume entitled *Drawings of Designs for Greenwich Hospital etc. by Sir Christopher Wren and Inigo Jones*. None of the drawings it contains can any longer be ascribed to Inigo Jones but the album does contain drawings by other important English architects including Wren, William Talman, James Gibbs and Edward Pierce, many of them of fine quality. Arthur Bolton (Curator from 1917 to 1945) noted that the volume was 'supposed to have come from the Wren Sale', but it is not clear how he knew this.

**Fig. 12**    This drawing from the so-called 'Wren and Jones folio' is for a monument to Viscount Irwin of Temple Newsam in Yorkshire, who died in 1688, and to his wife and his only daughter who died aged two. The design was never executed, a monument by John van Nost (d.1729) being erected in 1697 instead, in the Church of St Mary, Whitkirk, near Leeds. This sepia and grey wash drawing, which must date from the first half of the 1690s, is the work of Edward Pierce (c.1630–95). The cipher of interlaced 'Ts' on the lower right of the tomb and the characteristic gold border show that this drawing was once in the collection of John Talman (1677–1726). Pierce had stipulated in his will that his 'very good friend' William Talman (1650–1719), John's father, was 'to have the choise [sic] and picking' from his 'Clositt of Books, prints and drawings' and of 'what therein shall seeme to make up the worthy collection he intends', and this drawing must have been among those selected.

**Wren and Jones folio, f.61    396mm × 275mm**

**Fig. 13** This drawing in pen with grey and blue washes is attributed to Sir Christopher Wren (1632–1723) and bears the inscription *Sir Christopher Wren fe* in a later hand. It is thought to have been executed by Wren during his six months' stay in Paris in 1665 and shows a building with a Mansard roof which was a characteristic feature of much building in Paris by that date while it was not yet a form favoured in England. Wren was excited by much that he saw in France and brought back a large number of drawings and engravings. This drawing may well have been one of them. It is anyway an elegant design for an entrance façade in the style of a Parisian *hôtel* which would have had a courtyard reached through the gateway and a *corps de logis* beyond.

**Wren and Jones folio, f.20    450mm × 670mm**

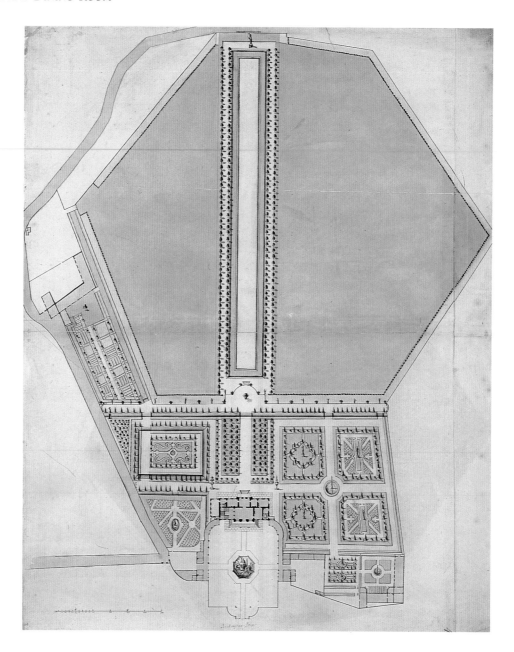

**Fig. 14** A third drawing from the 'Wren and Jones folio',
this time by Henry Wise, the famous garden-planner (1653–
1738). It is inscribed 'Buckingham House' – the older building
which forms the nucleus of the present Palace. In about 1702
the architect William Winde was probably carrying out
designs for the house originally supplied by William Talman
to the Duke of Buckingham. The plan shown is apparently
related to this scheme for which Wise was designing the
gardens. A survey of 1760 reveals that much of this scheme
was actually completed although the long canal was not
executed. This is a particularly attractive pen drawing with
colour washes.

**Wren and Jones folio, f.45    705mm × 560mm**

# THE STUDY AND DRESSING-ROOM

**Fig. 15**   A watercolour view of Soane's Study dated 3rd November 1825, looking southwards into the Dining-Room and Library. The red of the Dining-Room walls is carried on into this room, as is the green 'bronzing' which is used for the many shelves and brackets. There is yellow glass in the skylight and the floor is of bare pine boards, scrubbed so as to be almost white, which must have reflected light upwards. Most of the marble fragments shown here are still present. Many of those around the chimneypiece came from the Tatham collection (see Fig. 16) but the two cinerary urns to be seen in recesses just above the floor (there are another two on the other side of the fireplace) were bought at sales in 1801–2. Over the doorway into the Dining-Room is a large cast of 'The Apotheosis of Homer' taken from the original

marble relief formerly in the Palazzo Colonna, Rome, but purchased by the British Museum in 1819. The cast still hangs in this position. Some of the small items shown in the watercolour have been removed on security grounds. The bronze figure of Mercury on the chimneypiece now stands in the North Drawing-Room (Fig. 106). On the right can be seen Soane's pull-out desk which fits into the knee-hole of the fixed desk. This furniture was specially made for the Study in 1818 by Thomas Martyr. Above the chair on the wall hangs what is presumably the Mudge Chronometer (Fig. 91). Vertical Venetian blinds set in small hinged frames are fitted to the lower part of the window.

**Sketches & Drawings Volume (Vol. 82), p.18.**

**190mm × 200mm**

**Fig. 16**    Sketches of 'Various antique fragments collected at Rome for Henry Holland Esq., Architect, in February 1796' bearing the cipher of Charles Heathcote Tatham (1772–1842) and dated 'Rome 1796'. This is one of several sheets, now in the Museum, executed to show Holland what was being shipped back to England for him by Tatham, then his assistant and pupil. Most of the fragments collected date from the 1st or 2nd centuries AD and come from sites in Rome or those of Imperial villas in the countryside nearby. Soane had worked in Holland's office between 1770 and 1778 and kept in close touch with him afterwards. In the 1790s they collaborated over work on Government buildings and were both founder-members of the Architects' Club in 1791. Soane must have frequently seen Holland's collection of antique marbles on display at his house in Sloane Street. At Holland's death in 1806 they seem to have been bequeathed to his nephew, Henry Rowles, from whom Soane acquired them, probably with the intention of displaying them in the Study, his most personal room. Soane's diary records that he was busy 'arranging marbles' in the Study in the late summer of 1816 and two watercolours of the room in 1817 show Holland's marbles in place. The pencilled numbers against the items shown on this sheet are their Soane Museum Inventory numbers. The Holland/Tatham marbles still form the bulk of the exhibits in the Study today. Recently the marbles were cleaned and replaced in the very positions that Soane devised for them 175 years ago. The volume containing these Tatham drawings was acquired by the Museum in 1925.
**Volume 98, p.8    344mm × 254mm**

Figures 17 to 22 are among the objects displayed in two showcases in the study. These were bookcases in Soane's day, holding a variety of printed and manuscript works on architecture, including the *Codex Coner* (Fig. 20).

**Fig. 17**  Model for a figure on the tomb of Michelangelo (d.1564). This terracotta figure, which still retains its original painted surface, is a model for the statue of Architecture, one of a pair (the other symbolising Sculpture) that flank the tomb in Santa Croce, Florence, designed by Giorgio Vasari in 1564. This figure was to go on the right-hand side but the composition was somewhat altered in the full-scale, marble version. It is the work of Giovanni Bandini (1527–94), for which he was paid in 1568. The model for the companion figure, by Battista Lorenzi, is in the Victoria and Albert Museum. It must be said that the charm of these two sketch-models was lost when their forms were translated into the somewhat sterile statues that one sees in Santa Croce today. Soane, whose first curator described this terracotta as 'A small Model of a sitting female figure (both hands broken off)', would have been delighted to know its true identity and that – of all things – it is in fact a figure representing Architecture.
**Museum number: A58    H: 35cm**

**Fig. 18**  Terracotta model for the statue of James Craggs (d.1721), Secretary of State, on his tomb in Westminster Abbey, by Giovanni Guelfi (*fl.*1714–34). The monument itself was designed by James Gibbs, the most italianate of all British baroque architects, and the pose of the figure, cross-legged and leaning on a vase, was the first in 18th-century England to derive directly from classical Roman sources, possibly antique statues Gibbs had seen while working in Rome under the architect Carlo Fontana or perhaps figures reproduced in Montfaucon's *L'Antiquité Expliquée*, of 1719. Guelfi was brought to London from Rome by Lord Burlington on his return from Italy in 1714 primarily to work on figures for Burlington House and his villa at Chiswick. He was probably employed on the Craggs monument because of Burlington's friendship with the poet, Alexander Pope, a close friend of Craggs, who composed the epitaph for the monument and seems to have taken a great interest in the work – supervising the progress of the model at all stages.

The original face of the model is missing but a new and rather unsatisfactory face of carved wood has been provided at some time, perhaps at Soane's request. Very few of Guelfi's small terracottas survive. Soane purchased the figure at Richard Cosway's sale in May 1821 for £1.1s. In the sale catalogue it was described merely as 'A figure resting on an Urn, in Terracotta'. Soane, therefore, did not know that his little figure was by Guelfi: this fact, and the Burlington connection, would probably have pleased him greatly.
**Museum number: MP190    H: 38.9cm**

**Fig. 20**   *Right*: The entablature of the Temple of Castor and Pollux, which was rebuilt by Tiberius in 6 AD as part of his new Forum at the foot of the Capitol in Rome. This is one of the drawings in the *Codex Coner*, a compendium of careful drawings, mostly with dimensions, of antique classical buildings and of buildings in a classical vein that were modern when the drawings were made in about 1515. A preparatory sketch for this actual drawing in the Uffizi in Florence makes it possible to ascribe the main body of the drawings in this codex to Bernardo della Volpaia, a draughtsman working within the Sangallo circle of architects in Rome. The Uffizi sketch bears corrections by Antonio da Sangallo the Younger, who was soon to become architect for the major enterprise of the day, the building of St Peter's. The small plumb-lines shown in the finished sketch shown here are reminders of how the measurements for such drawings were made.

The *Codex* was never completed but seems to have been intended as a record of exemplary architecture directed at a highly educated High-Renaissance public. It was in Cassiano dal Pozzo's Paper Museum, which became part of Cardinal Albani's famous collection in the 17th century when the drawings were inlaid and rebound. The drawings from the Paper Museum were acquired by the architect James Adam, for George III, in Rome and brought back to England. The *Codex Coner* remained in Adam's collection and was included in the sale of the collection of Robert Adam, his more famous brother, in 1818 where it was acquired by Soane for £5. 18*s*.

**Codex Coner, f.85 (Ashby catalogue number)**

**232mm × 167mm**

**Fig. 19**   *Left*: An Italian maiolica plate made in the important workshop of Guido Durantino at Urbino in 1535 as part of a large service, of which nineteen pieces survive. All are painted with mythological subjects and bear the arms of the High Constable of France, Anne de Montmorency (1493–1567). Montmorency was a distinguished soldier and architect of French policy in Italy, whose seat was at Écouen, north of Paris. Some of the main rooms at Écouen were decorated by Italian artists, but it is evident from this specially commissioned maiolica that Italian furnishings of all kinds were also ordered for the embellishment of this splendid château. This plate is inscribed on the back, *Le Piche favoleg/giano nella festa/di Baccho/in botega di Mo. Guido/Durantino in Urbino*, and the story depicted is that of the three daughters of Minyas from Ovid's *Metamorphoses*, Book IV, who refuse to observe the rituals of the feast of Bacchus and remain indoors busy with their usual tasks and telling stories, and who are eventually turned into bats as punishment. An illustrated edition of the *Metamorphoses* had been published in 1533 in Venice and probably influenced the decoration of the service.

**Museum number: B47   Dia: 25.5cm**

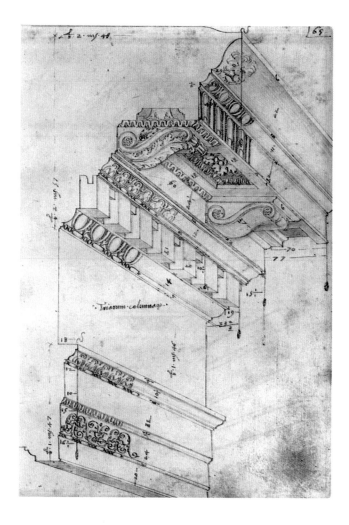

**Fig. 21** *Below*: An English medieval earthenware jug with slip decoration in the north French style. This handsome vessel is of what is known as 'London-type ware' and was probably made in or near the City of London during the first half of the 13th century. It is unusual in being made in two parts. It is one of several medieval ceramic vessels Soane apparently acquired from building sites on which he was working. With his strong antiquarian inclination Soane no doubt kept an eye open for such discoveries and acquired anything which appealed to him or seemed significant. This vessel, and others, were prominently displayed round the Dome in Soane's day (see Fig. 55).
**Museum number: M771    H: 31cm, Base dia: 12.2cm**

**Fig. 22** *Below right*: A German stoneware *Schnelle* (tankard) dated 1593. The first Museum Inventory, 1837, describes this piece as 'a Chopine . . . discovered in digging the foundation of a house in Bath Street, Bath'. A chopine is a liquid measure roughly equivalent to half a litre. A number of scraps of paper in the Soane Archive, all undated, refer to the purchase of this piece. The *Schnelle* is first mentioned as in Soane's collection in his 1835 *Description*, in which it is shown in one of the engraved plates, displayed prominently on the east pier between the Library and Dining-Room.

It was made in the town of Siegburg, near Bonn in the Rhineland, which was famed for the production of very fine, white stoneware unrivalled elsewhere. The *Schnellen* produced there were of an exceptionally high quality and are usually signed by a master potter. Soane's *Schnelle* bears the initials 'HH' (not visible in this view), for Hans Hilgers, who worked from 1569 to 1595. Many of these vessels were exported to England and this particular *Schnelle* was probably a special commission. Soane noted that it had 'belonged to the family of the Spekes of Hasleberry in Wiltshire as appears by . . . the armorial bearings with which it is decorated'. Beneath the figure of Venus shown here is a coat of arms incorporating the arms of the Speke (the two-headed eagle), Poltimore, Percy and Boleyn families. The central escutcheon is that of the Lord Treasurer of Wales, an office conferred by Elizabeth I on a member of the Speke family.
**Museum number: L73    H: 25.2cm, Base dia: 9.1cm**

**Fig. 23** Drawing by Canaletto (1697–1768). This must have been prized by Soane since in his day he had it framed and hanging in his Dressing-Room where it is still to be seen. It is a somewhat inferior version of a drawing in the Art Institute of Chicago. A recently discovered letter in the Soane Archive shows that this drawing was presented to Soane by Colonel (later Sir) Benjamin Charles Stephenson in December 1816. Colonel Stephenson was Surveyor General at the Office of Works (appointed after the death of James Wyatt in 1813) and therefore a colleague of Soane. He was later named as an executor in Soane's will. It is not clear whether he was the previous owner of this drawing or had acted as an agent. Whatever its origin the drawing has considerable charm. The view may be one of Canaletto's imaginary *capricci* but could be based on reminiscences of the little Italian town of Chioggia. The drawing is shown on the east wall of the Dressing-Room in a view of 1835 – where it still hangs today. However, at some earlier point Soane may have had it masking the aperture in the north wall of the Dressing-Room which opens on to the small adjoining lobby. The picture is of the right dimensions for this space and, when it was taken down recently, it was found to have a mirror in the back of the frame indicating that at some time the back was meant to be visible.

**Museum number: P18 (DR)    392mm × 292mm**

**Fig. 24**  *Opposite*: In the small courtyard outside these two small rooms there originally stood a striking feature, some 36-feet high, which Soane called a Pasticcio. It was erected in 1819 and was composed of capitals representing various styles of architecture, rising from a neoclassical base which came from Chiswick House (perhaps by James Wyatt) and topped by a cast-iron finial of characteristic Soanian form. The Pasticcio had become unstable by 1896 and was dismantled. This greatly reduced the significance of the Monument Court which was supposed to constitute an anthology of architecture. It would be a compliment to Soane if it could be replaced. Recently the architectural firm of York, Rosenberg and Mardell generously surveyed the surviving evidence concerning the appearance of this once dominant feature at the centre of Soane's Museum. They produced a scale drawing and a costing for reinstating the Pasticcio, a project which it is to be hoped will one day catch the fancy of a true admirer of John Soane. This watercolour, looking west from the Study or Dressing-Room shows the Pasticcio in the Monument Court on 19th August 1825.

**Sketches and Drawings Volume (Vol. 82), p.72**
**290mm × 192mm**

**Fig. 25**   A delightful Italian 17th-century bronze figure, perhaps of Venus rising from the sea (she sits on a shell and has a fishing-net in her lap), which served as the finial on the case of a pump that was apparently installed in the open loggia on the ground floor in front of the house until the loggia was enclosed in 1829. This pumped water up from a well in the basement. The wooden base may be part of the cover for the pump. Neither the exact position nor the appearance of the pump is revealed in any view or description of the front of the building.
**Museum number: MRR15    H (total):** *c*.37cm

**Fig. 26**   Fixed to the wall just outside the door from the Dressing-Room leading into the museum, is this figure of a female saint modelled in terracotta. It is probably the work of a Bolognese sculptor working in the mid-18th century, perhaps Antonio Schiassi (1722–77). Although damaged, this attractive object is yet another example of the catholicism of Soane's tastes which is seen here embracing north Italian rococo. This item was perhaps one of the 'terracotta fragments' bought by Soane at the Richard Cosway sale on 22nd May 1821.
**Museum number: M51    H: 34cm**

# The Corridor and Upper Drawing Office

**Fig. 27**  The space outside the entrance to the Picture Room is known as the Corridor. It has a long skylight which in Soane's day was filled with yellow glass, as can be seen in this watercolour dated 30th July 1825. When the plaster casts on the walls were white, the yellow tinge cast over them gave a pleasingly warm look. The walls were painted a stone colour. In the floor two grilles can be seen through which light penetrated to the Basement Corridor below. The staircase beyond leads up to the Upper Drawing Office (see Fig. 28). Most of the items visible here are still in the same positions, but the fine alabaster Roman cinerary urn on the right is now in the Crypt. A closely similar urn belonged to the famous 16th-century collector, Sabba da Castiglione, and is today among a handful of his possessions in the city museum at Faenza in Italy. In describing some of the objects in his collection, Castiglione maintained that his 'was undoubtedly the finest vase of alabaster' he had ever seen, 'even though I have seen many in Rome and elsewhere'. In the present Curator's view, the Soane vase is in no way inferior. **Sketches and Drawings (Vol. 82), p.84 281mm × 220mm**

**Fig. 28**   *Above*: This recent photograph shows the convex mirror and terracotta relief on the east wall of the Corridor. The mirror is visible in the watercolour reproduced in Fig. 27. A view westwards along the Colonnade is reflected in the mirror. To the right is an aperture which gives an unexpected glimpse through to the Nymph in the Picture Room Recess (see Fig. 43). Below the mirror is a terracotta plaque showing Britannia (seated on the right) attended by Peace and Plenty, with Justice in the background. It is an English late 18th-century work, perhaps by John Bacon the elder (1740–99). It could be the terracotta model for a fireplace relief. Below it is a plaster cast of a cipher, 'JMB', that was apparently 'part of the decoration of the ceiling of the Board Room of the Old Board of Trade Offices at Whitehall taken down in 1824 and refixed in the Board Room of the New Offices of the Board of Trade erected in 1826, on the site of the old buildings'.
**Terracotta plaque, Museum number: A81   34.9cm × 61cm**

**Fig. 29**   The buildings at the back of the site at 13 Lincoln's Inn Fields were designed not only to contain Soane's 'Museum' but were also where the offices of his active and highly successful architectural practice were located. Shown here is the Upper Drawing Office, installed in 1821 and then rebuilt again by Soane in 1824. Access to this office is via a staircase at the north end of the Corridor (see Fig. 27). The room is constructed independently of the main walls so that the two long skylights illuminate not just the drawing-tables but also the exhibits on the walls down to ground-floor level and even, on the north side, provide a ray of light right down to the Crypt. Soane described the Upper Drawing Office as 'peculiarly adapted for study. The place is surrounded with marble Fragments and casts, from the remains of antiquity, and from the Artists of the cinquecento; and the drawers are filled with architectural drawings and prints, for the instruction of the pupils.' At the far end, in the aperture, which Soane described as 'affording a birds-eye view of part of

the Museum', is a bust of Sir Thomas Lawrence (seen from the back; see also Fig. 55). Under the ceiling is a model of the vestibule Soane designed in 1798 for Bentley Priory in Middlesex; it is made without a base to enable the viewer to examine its vaulted ceiling (within) from below. Soane attached several models of ceilings and domes from his own designs to ceilings around the Museum.

This view gives some idea of the working-conditions of architectural draughtsmen at the beginning of the 19th century. In 1825 six men worked here, although George Bailey, the most senior, may have had a desk somewhere downstairs. They arrived at 9 a.m. and recorded their activities each day in the office day books, which survive in the Museum's archive. Much of their time was spent working on Soane's own designs (see Figs. 30 and 31) but they also made carefully drawn copies of pieces of antique ornament from Soane's collections, prepared lecture drawings (see Fig. 32) and visited sites to draw or survey.

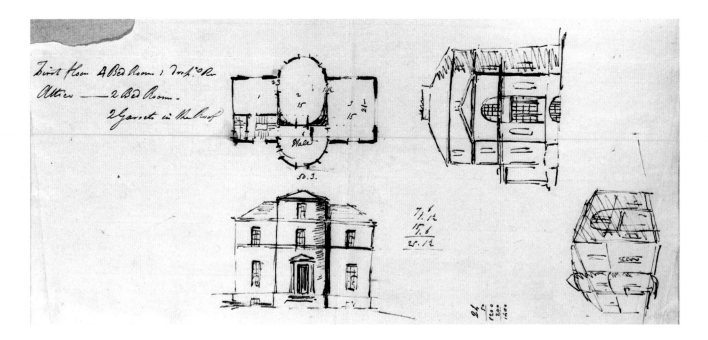

At this point it seems appropriate to reproduce examples of drawings generated by Soane's practice as an architect. There are in the Museum today some 8,000 drawings by Soane or from his office, including many vigorous rough sketches by the master himself, like Fig. 30. All the stages through which a project passed are represented and all this is complemented by models and by Soane's business papers which include a parallel record of all his buildings. No such complete documentation exists for any other architect before Soane.

**Fig. 30**   *Above:* When this drawing was made, probably in June 1784, Soane was still working entirely on his own. At this early stage he prepared the sketch and final designs and all the working drawings for his buildings himself. He also made all the site visits from London and acted without a clerk of works. These sketches are for the Rectory at Saxlingham, near Norwich, and are executed in sepia pen. Soane had already sent his client, the Reverend John Gooch, various proposals to choose from in March and April. These sketches are very close to the final, executed designs of June 1784. Work began on the site in July. In September 1784 Soane took on his first articled pupil, John Sanders, whose job it would have been to prepare the finished drawings, to scale, from Soane's rough sketches like the one reproduced here. This drawing is unusual at this date as it shows an architect working in plan, elevation *and* perspective at the inception of a design. Saxlingham Rectory survives and is one of the simplest and most geometrical of Soane's smaller houses.
Soane, *Original Sketches* (Vol. 42), p.37   195mm × 380mm

**Fig. 31** *Below*: 'View of the "Bank Stock Office" at the Bank of England – looking towards the North.' This fine pen and watercolour drawing is by Joseph Michael Gandy (1771–1843), 'the English Piranesi', who was the most accomplished architectural perspectivist of his day. He began work as a full-time paid assistant to Soane on Monday 8th January 1798, when Soane records that he sent him out 'taking plans in Grosvenor Square'. Soane soon discovered how skilful Gandy was at representing the effects of light in a manner not dissimilar from that used earlier by Clérisseau and Piranesi, and henceforth used Gandy solely for producing 'fair' elevations and perspectives.

This superb perspective shows the Bank Stock Office as built in 1792–4 and was probably partly made from sketches taken on site and partly from existing design drawings. Although dated 7th June 1798, we know from the day book that the drawing took seventeen and a half days to produce.

Gandy's drawings, as well as designs, working drawings and a scale model were important sources of information when the Bank of England decided to reconstruct Soane's Bank Stock Office within one of their banking halls dating from the early 1930s, a task accomplished in 1989. This totally reconstructed room is now the centrepiece of the Bank of England Museum and is open to the public.

Gandy worked in Soane's office until March 1801 but continued to work for him afterwards on a free-lance basis, producing a steady stream of brilliant perspectives many of which were shown at the annual exhibitions of the Royal Academy. Some of the finest of them are hung in the Picture Room and North Drawing-Room, where Soane himself placed them (see also Fig. 101).

**Drawing 11.4.1    570mm × 940mm**

**Fig. 32**    As Professor of Architecture at the Royal Academy from 1806 Soane prepared two important series of six public lectures. His first lecture was given in March 1809 and the last of the first series was delivered on 2nd January 1812. The second series of lectures was first delivered in February and March 1815. These twelve lectures were repeated over many years, with modifications and additions on each occasion. Soane appeared in person for the last time to read three lectures in 1821 but all his lectures were later repeated again annually by Henry Howard (the painter and Secretary of the Royal Academy) between 1832 and 1836.

To illustrate his lectures Soane had his pupils prepare, over the years, just over a thousand drawings such as that of Stonehenge shown here. Models were also used. In addition to being shown at the lectures the drawings could be seen at 13 Lincoln's Inn Fields the day before and the day after each lecture. They were the equivalent of today's diapositive lantern slides. Some are of poor quality, being copied from books, but a large number are based on survey sketches. In the present case George Bailey, Edward Foxhall junior and Henry Parke left London on 17th June 1817 to measure Amesbury House in Wiltshire and stopped at Stonehenge on the way back, on 21st June. Later in the year Parke prepared this finished watercolour and pen drawing and a large-scale plan from his survey sketches made on site. This drawing is dated 23rd September and shows the pupils engaged in measuring the stones. It is inscribed 'from the West looking Eastward'. Soane used this Stonehenge drawing to illustrate Lecture XII, on *Construction*, speaking of the 'mighty effort' required to move such immense blocks of stone. Henry Parke (1790–1835) was Soane's pupil between 1814 and 1820 and second only to Gandy (see Figs. 31 and 101) as a perspective draughtsman and colourist. Soane took Parke along as a draughtsman on his trip to Paris in 1819.

**Drawing 29.9.2    715mm × 1,275mm**

**Fig. 33**    Soane's own Museum retains its strongly domestic character although it is now a public building but very few of his truly public buildings survive. The most important of these is the Picture Gallery at Dulwich College which was built in 1811–12. This delightful drawing shows the lantern of the mausoleum at the centre of the Picture Gallery in which Sir Francis Bourgeois, and his friends Mr. and Mrs. Noël Desanfans lie buried. Bourgeois had bequeathed his fine collection of paintings, along with money for a picture gallery and mausoleum, to the college in 1811, agreeing before his death that Soane should be the architect. This drawing is by one of Soane's pupils, Robert Dennis Chantrell (1793–1872) whose initials with the date 'July 28 1812' are inscribed on it. Soane's office day book shows that Chantrell was on that day working in the office and actually went to Dulwich on 29th July.

Soane believed in the educational value of making drawings of buildings during their construction, maintaining that architects would be better able to 'ascertain the causes of a defect by attending the progress of buildings and by making Drawings of them in their different stages'. He expressed this view in one of his lectures, adding that the student would at the same time 'attain great skill in the mechanism of Buildings' and would 'discover many effects of light and shade, which close observation of Nature alone can give'. Consequently he often sent out his pupils, in pairs, to visit works in hand, to make views, which were then entered into a book recording the visible progress of the work. Chantrell was nineteen when he drew this picture (one of several such views of Dulwich) and had already been working under Soane for about five years. This view shows clearly Soane's use of yellow glass which was also a feature of many windows and skylights in his own Museum.

**Soane, Dulwich College Volume (Vol. 81), no. 14**
**220mm × 270mm**

# THE PICTURE ROOM AND MONK'S PARLOUR

In 1824 Soane rebuilt the adjacent house, No. 14 Lincoln's
Inn Fields, subsequently leasing out the front part but
retaining the plot of land at the back where he constructed an
addition to his Museum. This consisted of the Monk's Parlour
and Cell in the basement and a room on the ground floor to
house his best paintings. This Picture Room is one of the most
surprising features of Soane's Museum, with its huge swinging
planes installed so as to show many more pictures than one
would at first think possible in so confined a space.

**Fig. 35**  *Above:* This illustration shows part of the suspended ceiling which has the appearance of a late Gothic structure but without a single motif that one would normally associate with the Gothic style being present. The ceiling is now once again painted the colour that Soane used – a brown stone colour with a scumbled finish. The intention may have been to produce a Tudor or Jacobean effect in order to make this small room resemble an early cabinet of paintings; indeed, in the first guide to the Museum, published by John Britton in 1827, the room is actually called 'The Picture Cabinet'.

**Fig. 34**  *Opposite:* To John Soane as a student of architecture, the series of original ink and wash drawings by Giovanni Battista Piranesi (1720–78) of the temples at Paestum may well have seemed even greater prizes than his twelve Hogarths. Today they all hang in the same room but the fifteen Piranesis are massed inside the 'moveable planes' which are such a striking feature of the Picture Room. Thus assembled they make a powerful impression, as this view shows, and Piranesi's work did have a profound influence on Soane. These views of Paestum were subsequently engraved and published in 1778 by Piranesi's son, Francesco, forming a handsome volume, a copy of which is in Soane's Library. The small label of enamelled copper presumably dates from Soane's original arrangement of his pictures.

When he visited Rome in 1778 Soane met Piranesi (the year in which the great man died, shortly after having executed the Paestum drawings) who gave him four of his engraved views of Rome which were later hung in the Breakfast Parlour of No. 12 Lincoln's Inn Fields (see Fig. 94). Soane had been urged to call on Piranesi by Sir William Chambers who said the young architect should see him 'in my name', adding that 'he is full of matter, extravagant 'tis true, often absurd, but from his overflowings you may gather much information'. Later, when he was himself well established, Soane bought copies of most of Piranesi's works (there are eighteen volumes of his work in the Library), and he acquired at least two cinerary urns that had come from Piranesi's collection. The Paestum drawings were acquired in the 1790s but it is not clear where they had been before Soane secured them. Soane visited Paestum himself, twice, in January and February 1779. At that time he thought the massive Doric columns lacking bases 'exceedingly rude'. Nevertheless, he spent some time measuring the buildings and comparing his measurements with those published by Thomas Major in *The Ruins of Paestum* of 1768. Soane must have come to admire the ruins more as he grew older because, not only did he buy these Piranesi drawings, but he also acquired four large cork models of the same temples.

VIEW OF THE THAMES below GREENWICH. (SIR A.W. CALLCOTT.R.A.1779–1884.)

**Fig. 36** 'View of the River Thames below Greenwich', an oil-painting by Augustus Wall Callcott, RA (1799–1884) which also hangs in the Picture Room. The frame is original to the picture. This work shows the Royal Naval Hospital at Greenwich as seen from the Isle of Dogs but, as is typical of Callcott's work, the focus of the picture is the incident of genre – the fishermen – in the foreground. Soane commissioned the painting from Callcott for his collection of contemporary paintings in 1827 and it was exhibited at the Royal Academy in that year. It cost £84 which was quite a princely sum but by this time Callcott was becoming celebrated and Soane saw himself as a patron of the arts.

Callcott was much influenced by Dutch painting and by earlier English artists like Samuel Scott (1710–72). He was regarded by contemporaries as a rival of J.M.W. Turner; indeed, in 1813 Sir George Beaumont wrote, 'there is no way of knowing the pictures of one from those of the other'. Many of Turner's later works are of course very different in style but watercolours like his Kirkstall Abbey (Fig. 37) show why the two artists were regarded as equally talented in their portrayal of light and creation of atmosphere. Callcott was knighted in 1837, the year that Soane died.

**Museum number: P313 (MGR)    54.6cm × 85cm**

**Fig. 37**    A romantic view of the ruined Chapter House at Kirkstall Abbey, near Leeds in Yorkshire, painted by J.M.W. Turner, RA (1775–1851) in 1797 and exhibited at The Royal Academy in 1798. Kirkstall was a Cistercian foundation of the mid-12th century, the main buildings having been erected in about 1175. It was a picturesque antiquarian site much favoured by artists of Turner's day. This was one of several views which Turner produced of the ruins in 1797 but he chose this one for exhibition, perhaps because he had achieved notable success with a similar subject, *The Transept of Ewenny Priory, Glamorganshire*, in the previous year – one writer having described this as 'equal to the best pictures of Rembrandt'. The present picture was exhibited under the title *Refectory of Kirkstall Abbey, Yorkshire* although it in fact shows the Chapter House. After its exhibition it remained unsold until 1804 when, on 3rd May, Mrs. Soane recorded in her *Notebook*, 'Saw Turner's Gallery, bought a "View of Cormayer,

Vale de Aosta Savoy" cost £52.10s.0d, bought likewise "Interior of Kirkstall Abbey"'. We know from Soane's *Journal* that the Kirkstall view cost £36.15s.

Turner's friendship with the Soanes began in about 1802 and lasted throughout their lives. He probably met Soane first through the Royal Academy and was later Professor of Perspective (from 1805) when Soane was Professor of Architecture. Turner's early works, including this one, depict architecture extremely accurately. He also shared Soane and Gandy's interest in the effects of light. He was among the few close friends sufficiently privileged to be asked to stay at Pitzhanger Manor, Soane's country house at Ealing (see Fig. 41), where he and Soane went on frequent fishing-trips together. On several occasions Turner spent Christmas with the Soane family and he was the only person Soane chose to see over the Christmas following Mrs. Soane's death.
**Museum number: P312 (MGR)    50cm × 64cm**

**Fig. 38**   One of the chief glories of the Soane Museum is its two series of paintings by William Hogarth (1697–1764). These are famous and so much has been written about them that they are not discussed here where the intention is to draw attention to lesser-known objects in Soane's collection. However, the superb frames of the four paintings constituting the *Election* series, painted in about 1754, deserve to be as widely appreciated as the paintings they surround, and have surrounded from the outset. They are exceptionally fine expressions of English rococo carving and recent restoration revealed that much of the original gilding was still present; it can now once again be seen. The sludge green of the walls of this small gallery, a colour carefully selected by Soane, shows off gilding to great advantage. The detail of *Canvassing for Votes* reproduced here shows Hogarth at his most French, well aware of recent developments in French painting and especially of the charming genre-scenes of Pater and Lancret.

**Fig. 39**   *Opposite*: Sketch design for the ceiling of the Queen's State Bedchamber at Hampton Court Palace, by Sir James Thornhill (1676–1734), executed in 1715. The painting of this ceiling was presumably part of a redecoration carried out for the new Hanoverian king, George I, who had ascended the throne the year before. The subject of the central panel is Aurora, shown rising from the sea in her chariot. Night and Sleep lie below her. In the cove of the ceiling are portraits of the royal family. As shown here the portrait at the bottom is that of George I. In the completed ceiling painting this is over the bed and the king is shown crowned. At the sides are portraits of the Prince of Wales (later George II) and of his wife, Princess Caroline, while at the top is a portrait of their son, Frederick (later Prince of Wales). This sketch was thought by Soane to be for the ceiling of the Great Hall at Greenwich, the artist's most famous surviving masterpiece.

Thornhill's daughter married William Hogarth so it is perhaps not inappropriate that this oil-painting should today be hanging above no less than twelve splendid examples of the son-in-law's work (see Fig. 38). Moreover, alongside the Thornhill is a fragment of a Raphael cartoon for a tapestry (Fig. 40) and it is perhaps also pertinent to note that Thornhill spent no less than three years copying Raphael's *Acts of the Apostles* cartoons.

**Museum number: P126 (HR)**   **73.5cm × 64cm**

**Fig. 40**   Fragment of a tapestry design painted in tempera on panel, from the studio of Raphael (1483–1520). Pope Leo X ordered from Raphael a series of twelve designs (cartoons) for tapestries depicting the *Life of Christ* to go in the Scuola Nuova in the Vatican. The commission was supervised by Giulio Romano who was at the time working for Raphael. Tommaso Vincidor, another of Raphael's assistants, apparently executed cartoons for this commission in Brussels and it has been suggested that this head is by him. The tapestries themselves were woven in Brussels between 1524 and 1531 in the workshop of the weaver Pieter van Aelst and now hang in the Gallerie degli Arazzi in the Vatican.

The cartoons remained in the possession of the weaver and subsequently came into the hands of Govaert Flinck, a pupil of Rembrandt, whose son Nicholas (1646–1723) cut out heads, feet and hands and offered them for sale. Over a hundred such fragments apparently reached England in about 1720 and the painter Jonathan Richardson (1665–1745) owned at least fifty of them. In the sale of Richardson's effects

in 1747 the fragment shown here, the head of a youth from the *Presentation in the Temple*, was acquired by the Duke of Argyll. At the Duke's sale at Langfords' in 1779 it was purchased by John Flaxman the sculptor (see Figs. 54, 56, 58 and 88) and almost certainly came into Soane's collection via Miss Maria Denman, Flaxman's sister-in-law, between 1832 and 1835. Other fragments from the *Presentation* are at the Ashmolean Museum and Christ Church, Oxford, and in the Metropolitan Museum, New York.

Soane was extremely proud of this important object which, although Raphael himself probably never actually put his hand to it, is the product of one of the most talented teams of artists ever assembled at any period. The more famous 'Raphael Cartoons', those of the *Acts of the Apostles*, designed in 1515, were acquired by King Charles I and today belong to Her Majesty The Queen. They are now on display in the Victoria and Albert Museum.

**Museum number: P35 (HR)   55.4cm × 43.2cm**

**Fig. 41**    The pen and watercolour perspective view illustrated here, dated 7th November 1800, shows one of Soane's designs for Pitzhanger Manor, which was essentially his suburban villa, about an hour's drive from London and close enough to walk to from Lincoln's Inn Fields. Soane purchased Pitzhanger on 5th September 1800 for £4,500 and always maintained that he had rebuilt and furnished it in order to attract his two sons to architecture. This watercolour is by Joseph Michael Gandy (see Figs. 31 and 101). According to the office day book Gandy worked on this 'view of Ealing with the intended alterations' for thirteen days.

On the left can be seen the south wing which had been built as an extension to the original house by George Dance in 1768 and on which Soane had himself worked as a young man while in Dance's office. Soane retained this wing for sentimental reasons, but pulled down the older main body of the house in October 1800, replacing it with a rectangular yellow brick building, a design for which is shown here, very nearly as executed. Its west façade is modelled on the Arch of Constantine (315 AD) in Rome but relates also to the colonnade in the Forum of Nerva which can be seen in one of Clérisseau's gouaches in Soane's collection (see Fig. 42). Thus Soane suggested a link between himself and the architects of ancient Rome. Soane used the same formula for the Lothbury Court in his remodelling of the Bank of England (1797) which was swept away by the rebuilding of the 1930s. This must have seemed an appropriately grand frontage for the country

villa of the Architect to the Bank. The four Coade-Stone caryatids on the entablature at Pitzhanger were modelled from those at the Erechtheion in Athens, as were those used later on the façade of the Museum (see Figs 124 and 126). In this view Gandy shows the still unbuilt extension to the house in a realistic parkland setting. Soane took the laying out of the grounds very seriously and, as early as September 1800, sought advice from the garden designer John Haverfield of Kew who suggested a landscape with plantations, cedars in the lawns and a serpentine stream. John Haverfield had already worked with Soane on the layout of the grounds and bridge at Tyringham (see Fig. 122).

The Soanes used Pitzhanger mainly for entertaining friends. Soane recalled in his *Memoirs* the 'Gothic scenes and intellectual banquets' held there with up to two hundred guests coming to 'dejeuné à la fourchette'. Many of the works of art now in the Museum were first set out at Pitzhanger. By 1809 Soane's business had expanded to such an extent that he had very little spare time to spend at Ealing and it had also become obvious that neither of his sons had a serious interest in architecture. Pitzhanger was therefore put on the market and sold in 1810 and the contents were removed to No. 12 Lincoln's Inn Fields, which the Soanes had occupied since 1792, and to the embryonic museum that was beginning to take shape at the back of No. 13.

**Museum number: XP14    570mm × 970mm**

**Fig. 42**  *Opposite*: View of the remains of the Forum of
Nerva in Rome, by Charles Louis Clérisseau (1721–1820).
Soane owned twenty paintings by this influential artist and
architect who was a stipendiary at the French Academy in
Rome between 1749 and 1754, and thereafter became the
teacher of William Chambers, Robert Adam and Friedrich von
Erdmannsdorff, amongst others. He had a long and
complicated association with Adam and collaborated with him
on Adam's monograph on Diocletian's palace at Spalatro
(Split) in Dalmatia, published in 1764. Clérisseau was also a
friend of Winckelmann and Thomas Jefferson. Few of his own
architectural designs were ever built, but he had a great
facility for 'les morceaux de ruine' like the present picture, and
painted a monastic cell for Father Le Sueur at Santa Trinità
dei Monti in Rome to look like a ruined classical room
(*c*.1766). This survives and must have impressed Soane when
he was himself in the Eternal City between 1778 and 1780
because something of the same spirit – a classical setting
showing the ravages of time – was to be embodied by Soane
in many parts of his own Museum. The building shown in this
painting is the Templum Pacis in that part of the Roman
Forum built under the Emperor Domitian who died in 96 AD.
It fell to his successor Nerva to dedicate this new complex
which still bears his name (97 AD). Clérisseau's somewhat
fanciful impression of this part of the colonnade clearly had
great significance for Soane as he incorporated similar
columns into his design for the façade of Pitzhanger Manor.
**Museum number: P102 (HR)    61.5cm × 50cm**

**Fig. 43**  Plaster figure of a nymph by Sir Richard Westmacott
(1775–1856), a fellow Royal Academician and friend of
Soane's, and John Flaxman's successor as Professor of
Sculpture at the Royal Academy from 1827. A marble version
of this figure was formerly at Castle Howard, Yorkshire, but
was destroyed by fire in 1940. The marble was exhibited at
the Royal Academy in 1828 but this plaster version, which
may have been the full-scale model for the marble, was
certainly in, or envisaged for, the Soane Museum by 1823
when it is shown in its intended position in a watercolour
view of the projected Picture Room (constructed 1824–5). The
figure was then white. Soane paid Westmacott the sum of
£250 in May and June 1825, at around the time of the
completion of the building of the Picture Room, which was
possibly for the nymph. The subject has been described as 'A
Nymph unclasping her zone', which apparently means
undoing her girdle, but the Castle Howard figure was
described as 'Venus attiring herself after her bath', which
seems a more plausible title for the piece.

Whatever the case, one of the more astonishing features of
the Museum is to find this somewhat piquant figure standing
on her bridge, lit from above and behind, after first one huge
pair of doors in Soane's remarkable Picture Room, and then a
second pair, have been opened to reveal her. Indeed,
Westmacott himself was obviously impressed with the placing
of his sculpture since he wrote to Soane in January 1826 in
answer to a dinner invitation, saying, 'Mrs. Westmacott is
impatient to see the Nymph, since my account of the
compliment you have paid her'.
**Museum number: HR3    H: 153cm (approximately)**

**Fig. 44**   *Opposite*: Plaster bust of Georges Cuvier, signed on the back *P. Merlieux 1827*. Cuvier (1769–1832), although French, was born in territory then belonging to Württemberg and attended Stuttgart University. He was appointed assistant Professor of Comparative Anatomy at the Jardins des Plantes in Paris and subsequently permanent Secretary of the French Academy. In 1810 Napoleon commissioned him to report on the state of science and education in France, at which time he reminded the Emperor of the value of museums, which, he claimed, 'speak ceaselessly to the eye, and inspire a taste for science in young people'.

He became an energetic and highly successful propagandist for science in France, encouraging a massive popular interest in natural history, as well as building up his own very extensive library, which he encouraged the public to visit. He was involved in laying the foundations of a national system of education which has stood France in good stead ever since. He was indefatigable in his efforts to convey his message through lecturing and writing in a manner that has never been common among men of science, taking the trouble to study closely the powerful style of the famous actor, Talma, star of the Comédie Française, with the result that he enthralled his audiences. He was created Baron Cuvier in 1831. Soane must have been an admirer of Cuvier and certainly shared his views about the importance of education.

One of Cuvier's books, *The Animal Kingdom arranged in conformity with it's organisation*, of 1826, in English translation, is in Soane's Library (G.L. 36B). In the 1835

*Description* Soane records that this bust formerly belonged to Sir Thomas Lawrence (1769–1830), to whom it had been presented by Madame Cuvier, and also notes that it was said to be an excellent likeness.

The bust must have entered Soane's collection sometime between 1832, when Soane's *Description* does not include it, and 1835, when it was displayed on a table in the Ante-Room adjoining the Belzoni Sarcophagus along with several other busts. To the left of the bust in this view are two panels of German stained glass dated 1692 and 1695 from a Church in Cologne, while behind it is a wooden model for a lantern to go on the roof of Westminster Hall, designed by John William Hiort (1772–1861) when that important building was being restored in 1819–20.
**Museum number: M306    H: 36.5cm**

**Fig. 45**   Soane had many panels of ancient stained glass set into windows and doors in various parts of the house. Many, like the panel shown here, were removed later to protect them from the elements and the London atmosphere, or as part of James Wild's rearrangement of the glass in the 1890s. The subject of this German panel of about 1600 is St Judoc as a hermit in the desert (the German inscription confirms this – *in der Wusten Einsiedler*), an appropriate subject for the Monk's Parlour where it may originally have formed part of the decoration of the entrance door.
**Museum number: Panel 73 (Spiers)    17.7cm × 11.4cm**

**Fig. 46** A plaster portrait bust of Field Marshal Prince Blücher (1742–1839), probably modelled in 1814 when he was in London. At this time Blücher was universally known as the Prussian hero of the battles of Lützen and Leipzig, victor of a campaign against the French in 1814 and chief among those who entered Paris in March of that year and oversaw Napoleon's abdication and the restoration of the Bourbon monarchy. He was subsequently lionised in London. Turnerelli exhibited a bust of Prince Blücher at the Royal Academy in 1815, which was probably this plaster. With Napoleon's escape from Elba and return to lead the armies of France, Blücher continued to play a leading role in European history when he made his timely appearance in June 1815 on the field of Waterloo which led to Napoleon's final downfall. In 1816 Turnerelli used this plaster as the model for a marble bust produced along with one of the Duke of Wellington – presumably to mark their joint victory at Waterloo.
**Museum number: M119   H: 71cm**

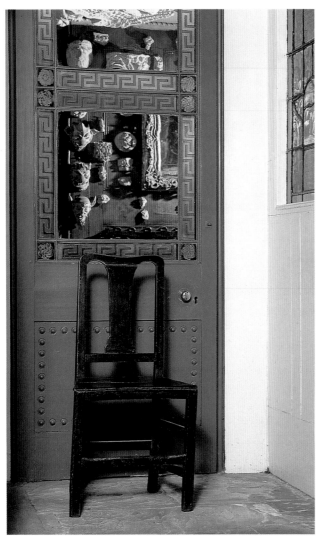

**Fig. 47** A niche at the foot of the stairs down from the ground floor, looking through to the Monk's Parlour and showing a bronze-green door filled with colourful glass – the one complete survival of the coloured glazing that was originally such a notable feature of Soane's building. The central panes are pale yellow and the key-fret borders are of red and clear glass with painted paterae in the corners. The stained pine chairs, today used by the warding staff, must be Soane's kitchen chairs, which are also comparatively rare survivals, such inferior furniture having almost always been used to the point of destruction.

**Fig. 48** *Right*: A view of 1827 showing the Monk's Parlour from the window side. The window of ancient stained glass, framed by what was then modern coloured glass, is reflected in two panels of mirror glass at the back of the room. More stained glass panels can be seen in the doors into the room and lining the niche to the left. The model of the Hiort lantern (see Fig. 44) is visible on the left, in the niche. In Soane's day the chest of drawers below contained the drawings made to illustrate his lectures at the Royal Academy (see Fig. 32). Low down to the right of the entrance door, fixed to the wall, is a 15th-century carved wooden triptych, now on the north side of the room. Above the bronze figures (one of these is now in a showcase in the Study) is a large model of the eastern façade of the Bank of England as built in 1823, now a very dark colour rather than cream, as shown here.

The woodwork of the room was evidently much lighter than it is today even if this lithograph cannot be taken absolutely

literally, and the green colour of the Picture Room, which was restored in 1988, may be seen above the model where the 'moveable planes' of that room are shown open. Yellow light is coming down into the Parlour through the coloured glass skylight over the Picture Room Recess. This view, executed by Penry Williams, appeared as the frontispiece to John Britton's

*The Union of Architecture, Sculpture and Painting, exemplified by a series of illustrations, with descriptive accounts of the house and galleries of John Soane*, published in 1827 – the earliest guide to the Museum which was superseded by Soane's own *Descriptions* of the 1830s.

**Fig. 49** *Above left*: A group of objects in the Monk's Parlour. In the centre on the left is a plaster cast of a misericord roundel from Henry VII's Chapel at Westminster Abbey, depicting a grotesque chained figure (possibly a bear) playing the bagpipes. Above and below are more casts of misericord roundels from Henry VII's Chapel. All are part of a large collection assembled in the Monk's Parlour and described by John Britton in 1827 as 'a profusion of Gothic fragments, trefoil and quatrefoil ornaments, foliage, busts, masks, small statues and other analogous decorations, many of which are from St Stephen's Chapel, Westminster and that of Henry VII, the Painted Chamber, St Saviour's Church, Southwark, and Westminster Abbey and Hall'.

All the casts shown here were probably made by Thomas Palmer and Sons in 1824, the year when the Picture Room and Monk's Parlour below were built and Soane was assembling pieces to fill the Parlour. This was conceived as part of a 'monastic' suite of Monk's Cell and Oratory, the Parlour itself and the Monk's Yard, with the ruined cloister and tomb, seen through the Parlour window, which was filled with stained glass. Soane's intention seems to have been to satirize the fashion for Gothic antiquarianism as well as produce what Britton called a 'truly picturesque' effect. The casts are not particularly well executed but enable us the better to recognise the excellence of some of the other casts in the collection, carried out in Italy by extremely skilled craftsmen (some from the workshop of the famous sculptor Canova) in the 18th and early 19th centuries.

**Fig. 50**    *Opposite right*: Wooden patera from the ceiling of the Painted Hall at Westminster; 13th century. This great hall formed part of the ancient royal Palace of Westminster; it was destroyed by fire in 1834. It was described in 1323 as 'that famous chamber on whose walls all the warlike stories of the whole Bible are painted with wonderful skill, and explained by a complete series of texts accurately written in French to the great admiration of the beholder and with the greatest royal magnificence'. The paintings were probably executed during the reigns of Henry III and Edward I. This great room was the king's State Bedchamber, a focal point of medieval palace ceremonial. However, in later centuries the room was gradually put to more public use and, by the 14th century, had become one of the first meeting places of Parliament. The spectacular paintings were later covered with whitewash and were only partially rediscovered in 1799 (when a drawing was made showing the flat ceiling studded with paterae like this one). It was not until 1818 that the chamber was properly investigated and recorded when the building was undergoing major alterations. Enormous public interest was generated by the discoveries, which were much featured in the press, and it must have been at this time that Soane acquired various fragments from the ceiling, including this flat roof 'boss' and a cinquefoil rosette. They were originally painted and probably date from a restoration of the wooden ceiling after a fire in 1263.

**Museum number: M363    45cm × 45cm**

**Fig. 51**    A fine terracotta statuette of Charles II wearing the robes of the Order of the Garter. This is the model for a statue that was erected on the Royal Exchange in the City of London, commissioned in 1684 by The Grocers' Company. The sculptor was Arnold Quellin (1652–86), a pupil and later partner of Grinling Gibbons; both were Dutchmen working in London. Unfortunately the finished statue, for which Quellin was paid £60 in December 1685, was destroyed by fire in 1838. However there is another model for it, a full-size head and shoulders, in the Victoria and Albert Museum. Soane acquired the model at Richard Cosway's sale in 1821 for £2.4s. and placed it in the Monk's Parlour. This purchase demonstrates once again the breadth of Soane's taste, the baroque exuberance of the figure embodying the very antithesis of the neoclassical ideal.

**Museum number: MP211    67.3cm × 30.5cm**

**Figs 52 and 53**    Two pages from Cardinal Marino Grimani's Commentary on the Epistle of St Paul to the Romans. This exquisite manuscript was produced by Giulio Clovio (1498–1578) who was responsible for the miniatures (the book contains several elaborate and very colourful compositions) while the elegant and astonishingly regular calligraphy in an italic script was executed by Clovio's assistant, Francesco Monteschi. Clovio had been trained by Giulio Romano (whose Christian name he adopted in favour of his own which was Giorgio) and apparently learned much from the miniaturist Girolamo dai Libri when they were both resident at the monastery of Candiana near Padua in about 1530. Marino Grimani, Cardinal of Venice and Patriarch of Aquileia (d.1546), was Clovio's most important patron and this work

was probably executed for him sometime between 1534 and 1538. A portrait in miniature of the Cardinal is among the decorations of this manuscript. The volume passed into the family library of the Grimani in Venice and was eventually acquired by Consul Joseph Smith who probably brought it to England. It was sold at Sotheby's in 1801 (the John Strange sale, 19th March) and then passed through several hands before being acquired by the Duke of Buckingham who included it in his library at Stowe in about 1822. Soane had built the library in 1805–6 and therefore knew the Duke who sold the 'Grimani Commentary' and two illuminated books of hours to Soane in 1833 for £735 – quite a considerable sum of money.

**Volume 143 (Millar 11)    350mm × 250mm**

**Fig. 54**   This skeleton and the wooden case in which it normally hangs came from the studio of the sculptor John Flaxman, Soane's close friend. Flaxman's library, auctioned after his death by Christie's in 1828, included many volumes relating to anatomical studies, in French and Latin as well as English. The skeleton likewise demonstrates his close study of the subject and was almost certainly used as a practical aid to his work as a sculptor. It was given to Soane sometime during the last six months of his life by Maria Denman (see Fig. 56) who included it in a list, submitted after Soane's death to the first Trustees of the museum, of items for which payment was outstanding. Although the skeleton had entered the collection during Soane's lifetime the Trustees, it is recorded in the minutes, 'did not think the skeleton and the skull of an animal were objects connected with the present Museum and resolved that a letter be sent to Miss Denman informing her that they would be safely returned to her'. Obviously, the skeleton was never sent back and it has remained in the Crypt area ever since. The skull is also still in the collection. The 1837 Inventory shows that at the time of Soane's death the skeleton, hanging in its cupboard, was displayed in the Monk's Cell.
**Museum number: M1490    H: (wooden case) 180cm**

# THE CRYPT

**Fig. 55**   The area beneath the Dome seen from the basement, with Seti I's great sarcophagus forming the central feature. In this view looking eastwards one can see the painted (marbled) balustrade supporting marble urns, on the ground floor, while beyond and above is the bust of Sir Thomas Lawrence, which in fact stands in front of an interior window in the Upper Drawing Office (see Fig. 29) that is tucked up under the roof. Soane later removed the coloured glass from the Dome and altered the shape to its present conical form. This wonderful watercolour by Joseph Gandy was executed in September 1825. Six months earlier Soane had celebrated the installation of the sarcophagus at the focal point of his Museum by holding three evening parties in March. The ground floor and basement were illuminated by candles and oil-lamps hired, at considerable cost, from William Collins, the stained-glass manufacturer, so proud was Soane of his acquisition which had in itself cost him the enormous sum of £2,000. The outside of the house was also illuminated by means of 256 lamps with glass containers for outdoor use, by John Patrick. More than 890 invitation cards were printed and the guests were served with cakes and tea or coffee. The servants were given ale and porter.

This alabaster sarcophagus was the outermost container of the coffin of the Egyptian Pharoah Seti I of the XIXth Dynasty (*c*.1300 BC); it is 2.45m long. It was discovered in Seti's tomb in 1817 by Giovanni Belzoni, an Italian strong-man turned archaeologist, and brought to England in 1821. The hieroglyphics carved over the whole surface, inside and out, were originally filled with a bright blue composition.

On the floor in front of the sarcophagus in this view are fragments of the lid, now on display in the New Chamber. The glass case which now covers the sarcophagus was put on in 1866 in order to protect it. This impressive antiquity is regarded as one of the most important ever discovered.
**Sketches and Drawings Volume (Vol. 82) p.47**
**390mm × 222mm**

**Fig. 56** Plaster models by the celebrated neoclassical sculptor John Flaxman (1753–1826), a great personal friend of Soane. Like Turner, Flaxman was a fellow Royal Academy Professor. The first Chair of Sculpture was created for him in 1810 and he held it until his death. He and his wife Nancy Denman, and sister-in-law Maria Denman, were frequent visitors to Lincoln's Inn Fields and to Pitzhanger Manor. The two families were on such good terms that Mrs. Flaxman was able to write to Mrs. Soane during an attack of rheumatism that if she should be laid up for two or three months she is 'determin'd to come to the Gouty Man in Lincoln's Inn Fields to be nursed – for my husband will having nothing to say to a Gouty Wife – do you agree to this?' Most of the more than sixty Flaxman models in the Museum were given or sold to Soane by Maria Denman after the sculptor's death. This handing over of material continued from the late 1820s until after Soane's own death (see Fig. 54). An even larger number of models passed via Maria Denman to University College, London. On the right in this view is 'Maternal Tenderness', the plaster model for the marble monument to Lady Fitzharris and her children in Christ Church Priory, Hampshire (1817). There are other models for the same monument at University College. This is one of Flaxman's few free-standing monuments. It was commissioned by Viscount Fitzharris after his wife's death in September 1815. Flaxman began work on the monument in 1816 and it was completed the next year. With Lady Fitzharris are her sons, James, Edward and Charles; several sketches of the boys made by Flaxman from life survive. Flaxman's natural treatment of figures was unusual at the time except perhaps in the work of Banks (see Fig. 57) and his work inspired many later sculptors, notably Chantrey (see Fig. 77). Flaxman may well have seen a Renaissance origin for this monument in the mother and child groups of Michelangelo, Raphael and Correggio, on which he laid great stress in his lectures. Sir Thomas Lawrence, in his 1826 discourse paying tribute to Flaxman, mentioned particularly 'the inimitable groups of childhood and maternal affection'.
**Maternal Tenderness,**
**Museum number: MRR11**
**H: 61cm**

MATERNAL TENDERNESS (J. FLAXMAN. R.A.)

**Fig. 57** *Above*: Original plaster model by Thomas Banks (1735–1805) for the figure of Penelope Boothby on her marble monument in Ashbourne Church in Derbyshire. She died in 1791 aged six and when, two years later, this model was exhibited at Somerset House it was greatly admired. Queen Charlotte and her daughters were among those who were moved to tears by this simple figure, 'drenched with sentimentality' as an eminent authority later put it, the child 'not dead but alive and sleeping', in which 'the theme of Innocence is exploited to the full'. If anything the plaster in the Museum is even more touching than the marble figure on the finished monument. The model was presented to Soane by the sculptor's daughter, Mrs. Forster, in 1830. She wrote to a friend on 13th April that 'in a few days the Model of the Child of Sir B[rook] Boothby will be in the Gallery of Soane'.
**Museum number: M44    30cm × 113cm**

**Fig. 58** *Below*: This marvellous plaster relief by John Flaxman is the model for a monument to Mrs. Helen Knight who died in 1801. Her tomb is in the church at Wolverley in Worcestershire. The relief is erroneously described in the 1837 Inventory as being the model for a monument to Mrs. Samuel Knight at Milton Church in Cambridgeshire. This relief is an especially fine example of a genre in which Flaxman excelled. Although the effigy is in contemporary dress, the pose derives from the figures to be seen on Etruscan sarcophagus lids and perhaps also from late Gothic sculpture like Arnolfo di Cambio's *Madonna della Natività* in Florence. Flaxman would have seen such work when he was in Italy between 1787 and 1794. The truth of Flaxman's claim that 'sentiment is the life and soul of fine art' should be judged when viewing this elegant and moving memorial.
**Museum number: M217    50.8cm × 87.1cm**

**Fig. 59**  *Opposite*: A view of the Basement Ante-Room with a plaster cast of *Venus at the Bath* in the centre. There is a large number of antique marble versions of this subject – all probably copies of a lost statue which stood in one of the temples of the Portico d'Ottavia in Rome and was mentioned by Pliny. The type was very much admired in the 18th and 19th centuries. The most noted antique version is that now in the Uffizi in Florence which belonged to the Medici family, but the Soane cast seems to have been taken from another antique version excavated at Salone in the second half of the 18th century and now in the Museo Pio-Clementino in the Vatican. There is a marginal note in the earliest Soane Museum Inventory, 1837, linking this cast with the Vatican version which has a bare right arm, whereas the Uffizi version wears a bracelet. Soane acquired this cast from the effects of the painter George Romney (1734–1802), sold at his home in Hampstead on 5th May 1801. Romney may have acquired the cast during his time in Italy, 1773–5. He had a recommendation to the Pope and was given permission to

erect scaffolding in the Vatican to help him make copies of Raphael's work. He would certainly therefore have been familiar with the marble there. Soane records in his Journal, 1801, that he paid Christie, the auctioneer, on 21st May, £5. 5s. 'for the Crouch. Venus' and it has always been referred to as 'The Crouching Venus' at the Museum. It is interesting that the plaster is painted black to make it look like a large bronze. On the wall behind is a large plaster cast of a Hellenistic marble relief of Perseus and Andromeda in the Capitoline Museum in Rome that belonged to John Flaxman.
**Museum number: M364    Crouching Venus, H: 87.5cm**

**Fig. 60**  A spirited marble relief of a lion-footed griffin from the end of a Roman sarcophagus, probably dating from about the 2nd century AD. This is one of the most striking of Soane's marbles although the carving is fairly perfunctory, as one would expect of such a series-produced and stereotyped item.
**Museum number: M61    84cm × 71cm**

**Fig. 61** This engraving depicting a guide showing a tourist the inside of 'a Sepulchral Vault in the Vigna Casali on the right of the Via Appia' is in a book in Soane's Library entitled *Via Appia illustrata ab urbe Roma ad Capuam*, published in Rome in 1794. It shows the kind of circumstances in which many of the items housed in Soane's Crypt were probably found and which Soane no doubt wanted to recreate in the gloomy basement at No. 13 Lincoln's Inn Fields. The book is dedicated to Sir Richard Colt Hoare (1759–1838), the celebrated banker and antiquary. The twelve engraved plates are by Carlo Labruzzi (1748–1817), an Italian painter who specialised in views of Rome and its environs. In 1789 Labruzzi was to have produced with Colt Hoare a large book on the monuments along the Via Appia between Rome and Capua. Unfortunately bad weather prevented them from completing their journey (although Labruzzi did make more than four hundred drawings) and the slim volume from which this evocative scene is taken was the only fruit of their enterprise. The inscription on another drawing in Soane's collection, a view across fields to St Peter's in Rome, signed by Labruzzi, suggests that Soane met the artist while he was in Rome in 1779. Soane also owned a copy of Colt Hoare's *A Classical Tour through Italy and Sicily . . .* (1819). Soane was obviously very interested in the ancient tombs flanking the Via Appia which he had travelled along several times; he included four drawings of such tombs in his lecture illustrations (see Fig. 33).

**Library Reference AL30     382mm × 583mm**

**Fig. 62**    Lid from an Egyptian mummy-case of about 1250 BC. This is merely a dilapidated wooden core; all the surface coating and paintwork have long since disappeared. Nevertheless, in 1840 (and presumably in Soane's day) this battered relic was thought to be 'of singular form and workmanship', and it may indeed have an interesting history. It was formerly in 'the gallery of the Duke of Richmond at Whitehall' and it came to Soane through the architect John White (see also Fig. 73). In 1758 the third Duke of Richmond put on display his collection of plaster casts of antique sculpture at his house in Whitehall in a gallery which was later decorated by Sir William Chambers. The gallery was opened to students of painting and sculpture who could receive instruction and compete for a silver medal twice a year. In many respects, therefore, the Duke's gallery was a forerunner of Soane's own institution. The building was destroyed by fire in 1791 but most of the contents were saved, some going to the Royal Academy which by this time had its own schools, and the remainder being removed to the Duke's country residence at Goodwood. Presumably the mummycase was among the objects displayed in the gallery.

The Duke may have acquired this venerable object when he was travelling in Egypt or he may have bought it at the sale, in 1766, of some of the effects of that intrepid traveller, Richard Pococke, who became Bishop of Ossory. Some Egyptian antiquities, including 'a wooden face of a mummy coffin [and] the skull of a mummy filled with embalming matter or mumia', were among the items sold. There is in the Museum a mummified head of about the right period (not on display) which may have been the 'skull' in question and therefore could be the companion piece to the coffin-lid. Pococke did anyway send to the Duke's father, in the 1730s, another mummycase and had arranged, in 1742, for the unwrapping and examining of an actual mummy before the Egypt Society at a meeting held at the second Duke's house. All we can say for certain is that the Museum's wooden lid (and possibly also the head) came from the collection formed by two influential and enthusiastic antiquarians, father and son, and that Soane had some reason to regard it as important.
**Museum number: M516    183cm × 55cm × 30.5cm**

**Fig. 63**   Head of a queen. This is one of four rather attractive plaster heads (two queens and two kings) which must surely be Soanean Gothic (about 1820). They have a Regency air about them even if the intention is to produce a medieval image. Soane did, of course, work in the neo-Gothic style, notably at the House of Lords (his work was destroyed in the fire of 1834) and at Stowe where he created a charming Gothic library and vestibule (1805–6), and even though he greatly preferred the classical idiom he knew perfectly well how to handle Gothic. He was nevertheless a child of his times and his approach to it was no doubt seen as somewhat dilettante by later generations of Gothicists who tended to require something altogether more robust. Several more plaster heads in this style are in the Museum, grotesque rather than, as here, graceful, and can be seen on the walls of the Monk's Parlour which of course contains an anthology of Gothic ornament of all dates, from medieval to Regency (see Fig. 49).
**Museum number: SDR3    36cm × 37cm × 26cm**

Beyond the main part of the Crypt, in the New Chamber, are displayed several cork models, of which Figs. 64, 65 and 66 are examples. Although the technique of making cork models of buildings dates back to the early 16th century, Augusto Rosa (1738–1784) is thought to have been one of the first artist-modelmakers, in the second half of the 18th century, to make cork models of antique buildings in Italy for foreign visitors. Other leading artists in this genre followed, notably Giovanni Altieri (see Fig. 81) and Antonio Chichi.

Although very few are known to survive in Britain today, a cork model of an antique building must have been a familiar feature of any interior bent on conveying a range of classical effects. Soane owned fifteen cork models.

**Fig. 64**   Cork model of an 'Etruscan' tomb, excavated at Nola, near Naples in southern Italy. This was made by Domenico Padiglione who, from about 1804, made models in the Naples Museum. Many of his models were sold through a dealer named Signor Gargiulo. Soane owned four such models but one of them was recorded as damaged in the 1837 Inventory and only the lid now survives. Soane purchased this model from the sale of Lord Berwick's effects in 1827 for £2. 14s.; nothing is known of the provenance of his other three tomb models. Originally displayed on the ground floor, Soane later moved them into the Crypt where they joined the 'Belzoni' sarcophagus, the Egyptian mummy-case and other mementoes of death with which he filled this intentionally rather gloomy part of his Museum. In his day it cannot have been easy to see the interior details of these models, in each of which lies a miniature skeleton surrounded by what Soane called 'a variety of Etruscan vases and implements of sacrifice' and with spirited paintings of Etruscan warriors on the walls. Research has shown that these models are very accurate and detailed records of what was discovered during excavations. The vases in this model are known to be exact reproductions, on a very small scale, of the originals which later entered Sir William Hamilton's collection.
**Museum number: M1078    21.5cm × 73.7cm × 40.7cm**

**Fig. 65**  A cork model of the Temple of Fortuna Virilis (late 2nd century BC) in the Forum Boarium, Rome, probably made in the late 18th century. Since the Middle Ages this temple has served as a church under the name of Santa Maria Egiziaca.

Many popular 'shows' in 18th- and 19th-century London featured models as part of their displays but only one devoted itself almost entirely to models – Richard Dubourg's Classical Exhibition. Dubourg opened his display in the 1770s and was prepared to sell items from it. Advertisements describe its 'elegant cork models of the most celebrated monuments of Grecian and Roman taste' including the Colosseum and the Temples of Paestum as well as Stonehenge and Windsor Castle. Soane visited Dubourg's on 11th March 1785. A month later the exhibition burned down during an experiment with a model showing Vesuvius erupting but another model emporium with a homonymous proprietor named Dubourg was opened in Duke Street near Manchester Square by 1798. A catalogue in the Victoria and Albert Museum shows that this exhibition also contained several exhibits duplicated in Soane's collection. Illustrations show that Dubourg's display was very similar to that of Soane's Model Room, set up in the late 1820s and dismantled after his death. This model shows the Temple of Fortuna Virilis standing on a rocky hill which is topographically incorrect but dramatises and romanticises the subject. A faithful model of the same subject by Chichi is in the Hessische Landesmuseum, Darmstadt and our model may be an English copy of this but with the base made more dramatic. It may well have come from Dubourg's 'show' where its romantic and dramatic quality would have been ideal. Dubourg did purchase a model of this temple from a Dr. Lettsom in the early 19th century.

One copy of the 1837 Inventory of the Museum lists this model as 'formerly in the possession of Mr. Tatham', presumably Charles Heathcote Tatham (see Fig. 16). In 1832 Soane paid Mr. Foxhall £8. 6s. for 'cork models from Mr. Tatham' and it seems likely that these included the present model and that of Stonehenge (see Fig. 66). Both are to be seen in a sketch of 1835 displayed on what looks like a purpose-built stand, with Fortuna Virilis above and Stonehenge below.

**Museum number: M1274    69.8cm × 73.6cm × 113cm**

**Fig. 66**    Cork model of the famous Neolithic stone circle at Stonehenge, in Wiltshire, probably made in the 1790s but certainly before 1797 (when a large trilithon shown standing in this model fell). The antiquarian John Waltire made two cork models of Stonehenge before 1794, one showing it 'in it's late state', (as it appeared in the early 1790s) and one showing it in 'perfect state' (a conjectural reconstruction). There is a possibility that Soane's model is Waltire's 'late state' model, but the arrangement of the stones in the model differs from that shown in a diagram in a manuscript in Soane's collection, entitled *Notes of Mr. Warltire's* [sic] *lectures at Birmingham, 1788, on Air, optical instruments, architecture* and labelled 'Plan of Stonehenge in its present state'. This model is, like the Fortuna Virilis model, supposed previously to have belonged to Charles Heathcote Tatham and was probably purchased with it in 1832. It may also have come from Dubourg's exhibition in which there was certainly a model of Stonehenge in the 1770s.

Soane shared an interest in Stonehenge with his friend John Britton (see Fig. 48) who owned a specially designed cabinet on which were displayed two plaster models of Stonehenge ('at present' and 'reconstructed') and one of Avebury, made by Henry Browne, 'Lecturer on Ancient and Modern History' and first Guardian of Stonehenge. Britton encouraged Browne's modelmaking and in 1826 planned the formation of 'The Druidical Antiquarian Society' which he hoped would turn Mr. Browne's 'abilities . . . to some account, whereby he might be personally benefitted and laudable curiosity be gratified'. Britton's own cabinet, which has been in the possession of the Wiltshire Archaeological Society since 1853, may owe something to Soane. The model on the top is under a glass case – each side of which is of a different colour, either clear, pale yellow, orange or red. This feature may relate to Britton's 'novel plan for exhibiting models and pictures to be elucidated by lectures' which was part of his plans for the future of the Druidical Antiquarian Society. He was already familiar with public spectacles of a theatrical nature like the Panorama, Cosmorama, Diorama and the Eidophusikon, all of which could involve coloured light, transparencies and painted scenery, and had himself given dramatic monologues at the Eidophusikon.

There is no evidence that Soane was directly involved in any of Britton's schemes although he must have known of them, and he was greatly interested in Stonehenge. In 1817 three of his pupils surveyed the monument and produced five large drawings – plans and views – for use as lecture drawings (See Fig. 32) along with an enlarged copy of Inigo Jones' plan of Stonehenge. In addition, Soane's Library contained a number of books about Stonehenge including Inigo Jones' *The most notable antiquity of Great Britain, vulgarly called Stoneheng, [sic] restored*. Interestingly Soane also owned a copy of William Stukeley's *Stonehenge, a temple restor'd to the British Druids* (1740) and his companion volume on Avebury. As a young man William Stukeley (1687–1765) compiled outstandingly accurate records of these great monuments but in later life became obsessed by the idea of the Druids, creating a whole mythology around them which led to the founding of the Ancient Order of Druids in 1781 and still influences people today. Unfortunately, we have no record of Soane's reaction to his ideas.

**Museum number: M300    19.5cm × 79cm × 79cm**

# THE COLONNADE

On either side of the central passage-way through the Colonnade stand two cupboards made up with doors in the style characteristic of the celebrated architect William Kent. The doors may have come from Walpole House (see Fig. 82). The cupboards are inscribed 'Drawings by the late Mr. Robert Adam', on their fronts and formerly contained the large collection of drawings (some 8,856) from Adam's drawing office which Soane acquired in 1833 for £200. This is by far the largest group of Adam drawings in existence and represents every phase of this famous architect's career and most of the projects on which he was engaged. The drawings are now in the Research Library.

**Fig. 67**   The present design is a full-size working drawing for a pier table to go in one of the main rooms at Apsley House, which Adam built in the 1770s for the Earl of Bathurst. The

house survives but was altered during the occupancy of the first Duke of Wellington. Like any good architect who cared about the finished appearance of the main rooms in houses he had designed, Adam would design all the chief items of furniture, especially pier glasses and the associated pier tables, of which this is an example. Many preliminary sketches for such furniture survive but full-scale designs have nearly always been ruined by ill-treatment in the workshops of the craftsmen who had to execute the actual work, so in consequence are very rare. The strong colouring of this design for a painted table will surprise many people who find it difficult to believe that 18th-century interiors could ever have been as brightly coloured as this design indicates. There are several more full-scale designs in the collection, one of them being even more brilliantly coloured.
**Adam Volume 49, 46    880mm × 600mm**

**Fig. 68** A single volume of drawings, which has only recently been attributed to Robert Adam, was acquired by Soane much earlier than the main collection, in 1818, at the Christie's sale of Adam's effects after his death (lot 53). The volume contains drawings of the antiquities of Rome and the surrounding countryside by Adam, Clérisseau and Lallemand, and some drawings of Neapolitan subjects made during a sketching trip in April 1755. Adam had left Edinburgh for Rome in 1754 and arrived there by the beginning of 1755. The sepia pen drawing on the lower left, one of the most evocative in the volume, is inscribed 'Sketch from my window in palazzo Guernieri [sic]'. This was obviously made in Rome while Adam was staying at the Casa Guarnieri, a house long patronised by English *milordi*, accompanied by Charles Louis Clérisseau who acted as his *cicerone* and drawing-instructor. The main sketch at the top of this sheet may be a design exercise produced at Clérisseau's behest. It seems to be a rather theatrical fantasy on an antique theme, perhaps inspired by a vanished antique building such as the large circular tomb situated between Gallicano and Hadrian's Villa which Adam could have known only from plans drawn during the late 16th century by the architect-antiquarian Pirro Ligorio when the building was already ruined, although traces of painting and stucco apparently then still remained. The small topographical sketch on the lower right here is as yet unidentified. The volume is inscribed 'Sketches and Drawings of Places and Views in Italy taken on the spot by different hands'.
**Volume 7: 150, 151 and 152    Sheet size 620mm × 490mm**

**Fig. 69** This charming design by Robert Adam is pasted on to the same page as another inscribed 'Sketch of a Hutt for the Honble Miss Curzon at the upper end of the garden at Kedleston'. In the 1760s and early 1770s Adam designed a range of garden buildings, and 'eye-catchers' for the grounds at Kedleston, Nathaniel Curzon's seat in Derbyshire, which included a Fishing-Room, a Grotto or Rock Room, a Pheasant House, a Hermitage, a View Tower and a Thatched Cottage. It is probable that the present design dates from the same period although it does not seem to have been executed. In some respects it resembles the Fishing-Room (*cum* Boat House and cold bath) which survives. The Miss Curzon of the inscription would have been Caroline (*c.*1753–1841) elder daughter of Nathaniel Curzon, who would probably have been about twenty at the time. The drawing shows an asymmetrical rustic building, a very early example of a type which was to become popular all over Europe in fashionable gardens and parks, and it must be at least a decade earlier than that most famous expression of this taste, Marie Antoinette's *Le Hameau* in the park at Versailles, which was not built until 1783.
**Adam Volume 1, 242    182mm × 318mm**

**Fig. 70** Marble statue of the Ephesian Artemis or Diana. Although much restored the torso is an antique Roman adaptation of a wooden cult figure which it is believed once stood in the Temple of Artemis at Ephesus in Asia Minor. Many statues of this type were produced in the Graeco-Roman region and this one dates from the second half of the 2nd century AD. This statue may well be that mentioned by Cartari, writing in 1647, as having been excavated in Rome under Pope Leo X (Pope from 1513 to 1521) and is likely to have contributed, along with another in the Capitoline Museum, to the image of the Ephesian Diana which appears in the Vatican Logge, which were decorated in fresco by Raphael in 1518–19. The Soane figure may also be the one described by the antiquarian Ulisse Aldovrandi in 1550 as being in the collection of Cardinal Rodolfo Pio da Carpi in his garden *antiquarium* on the Quirinal Hill where the Palazzo Barberini now stands – one of the most important of all the 16th-century Roman collections of antiquities. A sketch and detailed description made by Boissard in 1559 show that the statue was by that time in the garden of the Villa Poggia which, with the neighbouring garden of the Villa Giulia, formed the *Vigna Giulia* – housing the extensive collection of Julius III (Pope from 1550 to 1555). Cardinal Carpi and Pope Julius enjoyed a mutual interest in antique sculpture. They apparently shared newly excavated sculptures and, on the Pope's death, Carpi received some pieces from his collection.

The Soane statue must have left the *Vigna Giulia* when the collection was broken up between 1562 and 1564. After the 16th century the whereabouts of the Soane figure is uncertain although it was engraved and published in Montfaucon's influential book, *L'Antiquité Expliquée* of 1719 which in itself confers distinction on it. Soane acquired it at the Earl of Bessborough's sale of 19th April 1804, for 61 guineas, and it is shown in a watercolour of the Dome area executed in 1811–12. By 1825 Soane had moved it to its present position in the Colonnade.

The antique marble torso is well preserved but the black marble hands, face and feet are restorations. Boissard's 16th-century sketch shows the statue with face and hands but his detailed description does not mention that they are black, in contrast to the rest of the statue. Therefore it seems probable that the black hands, face and feet are later replacements of earlier restorations. They were certainly in place by the time Montfaucon's engraving appeared in 1719. The top part of the turreted crown and other ornaments are probably the result of later 18th-century restorations.

**Museum number: M613**    123cm × 33cm × 21.5cm

**Fig. 71**    Fragment of a female figure of white marble from the frieze on the north portico of the Erechtheion, on the Acropolis at Athens (421–405 BC). Soane had no idea that this small figure came from such an important monument; its identity was established by Professor Bernard Ashmole in 1927. We do not know when it was removed from the portico or how Soane acquired it. However, the buildings on the Acropolis were gradually despoiled for centuries before Soane's time, as pieces of sculpture were hacked off by local people for tourists wanting souvenirs. George Basevi, one of Soane's pupils, wrote to him from Rome in 1819 in terms which suggest that his master may have been among those who deplored the damage caused by Lord Elgin's removal of large sections of sculpture from the Parthenon and the Erechtheion. Soane greatly admired these buildings and discussed them in his lectures with accompanying large-scale drawings made by his pupils for that purpose. He owned some fifteen casts of ornament from them and had models by Fouquet of both buildings (see Fig. 123). The two Coade-Stone caryatids on the façade of Soane's house are based on those on the Erechtheion (see also Fig. 41), and the same figures appear in Ward's portrait of Soane's pet dog (see Fig. 97). He would undoubtedly have been delighted to know whence this little piece of sculpture had come.
**Museum number: M321 (Vermeule 278)**
37cm × 14cm × 14cm

**Fig. 72**    A stoneware key-stone decorated in relief with the head of a river god. This imposing piece of architectural ornament is made of Coade Stone and was No. 438 (priced at £1. 11s. 6d.) in the illustrated catalogue issued in 1784 by Eleanor Coade, proprietor of the important manufactory of this remarkably stable and weather-resistant material, which she established in 1769. Like most of the prominent architects of his time, Soane frequently used ornaments of this material on his buildings (a copy of the original catalogue is still in the Museum); the pair of caryatids on the balcony on the façade of the house are noteworthy examples and show that Coade Stone also lent itself to the making of large objects (see Fig. 126). The sculptor John Bacon the elder (see Fig. 28) provided many of the designs produced at the factory, which stood at the southern end of Westminster Bridge, on the site of the present County Hall. Bacon is very likely to have produced this design which was perhaps inspired by similar aquatic figures on the 17th-century fountains in the park at Versailles.
**Museum number: M1130    H: 68.5cm**

# THE DOME AREA

**Fig. 73**    A watercolour dated 4th August 1825 of the Dome area at ground floor level, looking south. On the right is the large plaster cast of the Apollo Belvedere which came from Chiswick House (see Fig. 74). It will be noted that it was white in Soane's day, as were most of the marbles, urns and busts on the balustrade. The deal floor is scrubbed. Today the bust of Sir John Soane presides over this central area of his Museum (see Fig. 77). On the far wall (above, left) can be seen the marble pilaster capital from the Pantheon in Rome (Fig. 84). In order to show one end of the sarcophagus in the Crypt below, a marble urn in the foreground has been omitted by the artist.

**Sketches and Drawings Volume (Vol. 82), p.114**

**221mm × 336mm**

**Fig. 74** *Opposite*: View across the Dome looking west towards the over-size figure described in the Museum Inventory of 1837 as 'A Cast from the Antique Statue of the Apollo Belvedere, brought into England by the Earl of Burlington, and formerly in his Villa at Chiswick'. Apparently Burlington had the cast made in about 1719 from the original marble now in the Museo Pio-Clementino at the Vatican (a Roman copy of about 135 AD after a lost Greek bronze). The figure was later given to the architect John White (1747– 1813) by the fifth Duke of Devonshire, for whom White added wings to Chiswick House in 1788. White subsequently presented it to Soane, as the latter records in his 1830 *Description*. The Apollo was moved to Lincoln's Inn Fields in 1811, probably from White's house in Devonshire Place, St Mary-le-bone, and the bill for this survives in the Soane Archive, showing that at least seven men were employed on the job and that £1. 4s. was paid to a Mr. Mathews 'for canisters' (probably basket-work protection) to help in the move. The total cost was £16. 17s. 6½d. Soane wrote in his 1835 *Description* that he had 'set so much value on it, as to take down a large portion of the external wall in order to admit it into its present position'. Soane also designed the pedestal on which the figure now stands, which incorporates a small table.

Soane was very proud of this acquisition, for not only was the Apollo Belvedere at the time considered 'the highest and most sublime representative of ideal form and beauty' (*Report of the Select Committee of the House of Commons on the Earl of Elgin's Collection of Sculptural marbles*, 1815/16), but this particular version of it had the added glamour of coming from the collection of one of the key figures in English architectural history. Soane certainly knew all about Burlington's central role in the evolution of the English neo-Palladian style, of which the villa at Chiswick was the most notable expression of all. The original marble, from which Burlington's copy was made, had been assembled from fragments in the 16th century, when it was also provided with arms. In the 1920s the old repairs were removed and the pieces reassembled so that the figure now stands leaning back slightly and has no hands. In the foreground is the Chantrey bust of Soane (see Fig. 77) seen from behind. The panel below dates from the late 18th century, although Soane believed it was antique and described it as 'a Genius in a Triumphal Car, in Mosaic, found in Hadrian's Villa'.

**Apollo cast, Museum number: M875    H: 215cm (excluding base)**

**Fig. 75**    Cast of an embossed silver basin, decorated with merfolk celebrating the marriage of Neptune and Amphitrite; Italian, late 16th century. The original was formerly in the Church of Santa Barbara in Mantua but was removed by French Republican troops in 1796 and is believed to have been destroyed, probably through being melted down for its metal-value. This cast was one of a series made by Sigismondo Fabbrici shortly before that event. The central boss is a conjectural reconstruction, with a portrait of Carlo I Gonzaga, Duke of Mantua 1627–37. Other casts made from the same dish have a medallion of Santa Barbara on the central boss: neither are plausible in this context. The cast was amongst a collection formed by Lewis Wyatt in Rome in 1820, consisting mainly of casts of architectural ornament taken by Canova's workman, Benedetto, and sold to Soane in 1834.

Basins such as this were usually associated with a matching ewer and were used for washing the hands before and after meals on grand occasions. A servant armed with a hand-towel held the basin beneath the diner's hands and poured lukewarm scented water over them. This basin is reminiscent of Genoese goldsmith's work and would certainly have been executed in silver-gilt. It is an example of Soane's breadth of interest and sure eye for fine design. It is remarkable, none the less, that such a full-blooded composition, with its rolling baroque forms, should have appealed to a man of his generation, for it would seem to embody the very antithesis of that glacial quality so characteristic of most early 19th-century classicism.

**Museum number: M946    Dia: 53.2cm**

**Fig. 76**    John Soane at the age of twenty-one, a chalk drawing by Nathaniel Dance, RA (1734–1811). Executed in about 1774, some four years before he went to Italy, this shows Soane as the eager young architect, lively, intelligent and full of promise. Soane's wife had this hanging in her Morning Room, a small room on the second floor of No. 13 Lincoln's Inn Fields, which was essentially her private closet where she kept her favourite belongings. There are several other portraits of Soane in his Museum including the famous painting by Sir Thomas Lawrence executed in 1828–9 when Soane was an old man, but this little portrait and the bust shown in Fig. 77 are the most attractive.

**Museum number: P317 (MGR)    295mm × 210mm**

**Fig. 77**  Portrait bust of John Soane, executed in white statuary marble by Sir Francis Chantrey, RA (1782–1841). In May 1827 Chantrey wrote to Soane asking him to come for a sitting and 'to bring your head with you'. The bust was completed by 5th April 1829 when Chantrey could write claiming that 'I have at last persuaded myself that my labours are brought to be successful termination, but whether the Bust I have made shall be considered like John Soane, or Julius Caesar, is a point that cannot be determined by you or me. I will however, maintain that as a work of art I have never produced a better.' The bust is inscribed 'John Soane Esq RA Presented as a token of respect by Francis Chantrey, Sculptor, 1830'. It was exhibited at the Royal Academy in that year and subsequently displayed in the Tivoli Recess on the staircase before being placed in its present position at the focal point of Soane's Museum on the morning of 25th October 1833. Although it might seem that Chantrey was being exceptionally generous, he did in fact receive in exchange professional help from the great architect in the form of designs for an ante-room to the sculpture gallery at his own house in Belgrave Square. Apparently Chantrey was not too sure, at one point, that Soane would do his part, so sent a letter saying 'see you I *must* and *will* for the purpose of sucking your brains about the outside finishing of the Soannean [sic] Elevation'.

**Museum number: M931    H: 76cm**

**Fig. 78**  Portrait miniature of Mrs. Soane (née Elizabeth Smith) painted on ivory by William Dance (b.1737). Unfortunately much damaged, the portrait still shows us a bright-eyed, smiling and apparently lively young woman. John Soane recorded in his *Notebook* for 1784 that, on 4th and 6th May, he went with Miss Smith 'to sit for Mr. Dance'. Although it is recorded in the Bailey Inventory of 1837 that this miniature is by Nathaniel Dance, the celebrated portrait painter, it is more likely that it was executed by his brother William, who was a miniature painter. The posthumous portrait of Mrs. Soane by John Jackson, which hangs in the Picture Room, was said by Soane in his own *Description* of his house in 1835 to have been based on a drawing by Flaxman and 'a miniature by William Dance'. This miniature shows Soane's future wife at the age of twenty-four, just three months before their marriage. Soane's *Notebooks* first mention Elizabeth Smith towards the end of 1783 and chart a rapid courtship thereafter – with dinners and trips to the theatre and Vauxhall Gardens. In May 1784, just after the sitting to Dance, Soane ceases to refer to 'Miss Smith' and begins to refer to 'Eliza'. It was probably around this time that their engagement was announced. On the death of her uncle, George Wyatt, in 1790, Mrs. Soane inherited valuable property extensive enough for her husband to record in his *Memoirs* that 'my income was so increased as to render me independent of professional emoluments'. This miniature gives a very much more charming image of her than does Flaxman's rather dour drawing that hangs in the South Drawing-Room.

**Museum number: SDR 21.50    8.5cm × 6.7cm**

**Fig. 79**    A portrait of Mrs. Soane senior, the mother of Sir John Soane, at the age of eighty-four, by John Downman (1750–1824), dated 1798 and exhibited at the Royal Academy in that year. Downman was a fashionable society portraitist using the standard black chalk and watercolour technique but with his own trick of applying the flesh colours to the reverse of thin paper so that they show through very delicately. On 12th March 1798 Soane paid Downman £21 for 'the portraits of [the] Old Lady and John', namely this attractive picture and its pair, a portrait of John Soane junior, the architect's eldest son. There are preparatory pencil sketches for both portraits in the British Museum.

Very little is known about Soane's mother, to whom he evidently bore a striking resemblance. She was born Martha Marcy in 1714 and her bible, which survives in the Museum's library, records her marriage to John Soan, a builder, as having taken place on 4th July 1738 and that she was twenty-three at the time. John Soane was the youngest of her six children, born in September 1753 when the family were living in Whitchurch, near Reading. His social aspirations led him to add an 'e' to the family name in 1783, and he later acquired a coat of arms. Soane's father died in 1768, aged fifty-four, and is buried at Goring-on-Thames. By the time Soane began to keep his *Notebooks* his mother was living in Chertsey in Surrey, quite close to his brother William. The *Notebooks* record that Soane paid his mother frequent visits, especially after his marriage in 1784, travelling in his own carriage as far as Hounslow and then going on to Chertsey in a hired chaise. Elizabeth Soane may have assumed some responsibility for looking after things in her mother-in-law's household, since regular sums are recorded as being paid to 'Mrs. Soane, for Chertsey'. Soane's *Notebooks* also record that he paid his mother a direct quarterly allowance for some years and that he wrote to her regularly. On 30th January 1800 Soane recorded in his *Notebook*, 'Poor Old Lady died this day at 10 o'clock in the evening in her 87th year, without a groan!'

After old Mrs. Soane's death Soane's brother William continued to live in Chertsey and Soane supported him with an annuity until his death sometime after 1823. Soane also continued to visit Chertsey frequently, not just to see William but also to go fishing and visit other friends, who included the Smiths, a large family who may have been relatives of Mrs. Soane, and 'Mr. Peacock of Chertsey' – probably the novelist Thomas Love Peacock.

**Museum number: P296(MGR)**    37cm × 31cm

**Fig. 80**   Miniature portrait of a lady in its case; about 1640.
The costume helps us date this rather charming curiosity, an
example of naive painting which could have been executed
anywhere north of the Alps. It is published here partly for its
own sake but also in the hope that someone may feel they can
add something to the meagre information in the Museum's
files. The portrait is painted on wood which is set into a
wooden case. Miniatures of this class have not often been
preserved but may well have been relatively common in their
day.
**Museum number: S53    10cm × 13.5cm (open)**

**Fig. 81**    Cork model of the Temple of Vesta at Tivoli made by Giovanni Altieri at Naples in 177 . . . (the last figure is missing from the incised inscription on the plinth). Altieri made a similar model in 1767 for the Society of Antiquaries in London while he was still working in Rome. The dimensions of this model (now lost) and probably also of Soane's were based on measurements taken by Giovanni Stern (1734–94), an Italian architect who seems to have done his survey in collaboration with George Dance the Younger (see Figs. 102 and 103), for whom Soane later worked. After returning to Naples, his native city, Altieri continued to produce cork models of celebrated antiquities, like the present fine specimen and two showing ruined buildings at Pompeii commissioned by Gustavus III of Sweden, which are still at Drottningholm Castle. In the 1790s he was engaged by the Royal Porcelain Factory at Naples to provide models for some of their

products. The Temple of Vesta at Tivoli dates from the early 1st century BC. Soane took careful measurements of the building when he was in Italy as a student in 1778–9 and it was to remain a powerful source of inspiration in his own work throughout his career. He bought this cork model for £16 at Mr. Govan's sale in 1804 along with another, of the Arch of Constantine. In one of Joseph Gandy's most spectacular views of the inside of the Museum, executed in 1813, this model is shown perched on a tottering pile of architectural fragments that is balanced, Piranesi-fashion, on the edge of the parapet beneath the Dome at the centre of the Museum. In 1834 Soane also purchased a plaster model of a conjectural reconstruction of the temple made by Fouquet of Paris (museum number MR13; see figure 123).

**Museum number: MR2    39cm × 52cm × 50.5cm**

**Fig. 82**    One of a pair of very fine console tables in the style of William Kent (1685–1748) which came from Walpole House, Chelsea, demolished by Soane in 1809 to make way for the new Infirmary he had designed for the Royal Hospital. There is no record that William Kent worked for Sir Robert Walpole at Chelsea although his work for this famous Prime Minister at Houghton, in Norfolk, is rightly celebrated. This table and its pair seem to be so unmistakably in Kent's style that one must presume that he also did some work at Chelsea, perhaps in 1730 when Walpole purchased the lease. Whatever the case, these tables are small and must have come from a closet. They were probably originally grained to look like walnut but have at some point since been touched up with black paint. The marble tops on the two tables are not identical although both incorporate a display of marble samples. Several other items in the Museum also came from Walpole House, including a neo-Palladian console table in the Monk's Parlour which Soane adapted so that it would fit into a niche (see Figs. 48 and 67).

On the table are two lead figures of slaves after those by Pietro Tacca (1577–1640) on the monument of Ferdinand I at Leghorn (Livorno; see also Fig. 106). During the 18th century Tacca's originals were considered to be the work of Giambologna and were extremely popular. These reduced-scale copies are probably by an English sculptor, perhaps Caius Gabriel Cibber (1630–1700) who modelled two nude figures of 'Raving' and 'Melancholy' Madness for the gate of Bedlam Hospital which were certainly influenced by Tacca's slaves. Between the two lead figures is a plaster bust of Napoleon after Canova.

**Table, museum number: H23**    71.5cm × 111cm × 64.5cm

**Fig.83** *Previous pages:* One of the great treasures of the Soane Museum is this superb Canaletto view of Venice with the Riva degli Schiavoni on the right, San Giorgio on the left, and Santa Maria della Salute and the Doge's Palace in the distance. This is counted among the very finest of Canaletto's paintings of which many copies were made in his workshop. In 1736 Canaletto was paid 120 zecchini for a large view described as 'una parte di Venezia principiando a S. Biagio sino alla Salute' commissioned by Count von der Schulenburg. This was almost certainly the present painting. In 1741 the artist Piazzetta, always reluctant to recognise the talents of others, said it was worth 2,000 ducats. This was more than the value he placed on any other work by a Venetian artist of the time, including himself. The painting belonged at one time to the celebrated French finance minister, Charles Alexandre de Calonne, a highly discriminating collector of paintings who later came to live in England. The picture subsequently came into the hands of Alderman Beckford (1709–70) and was included in the sale of items from his house, Fonthill Splendens, in 1807 (lot 605) when Soane purchased it for £157.10s.

**Museum number: P66 (HR)   122cm × 200cm**

**Fig. 84**   'A Capital of a pilaster from the interior of the Pantheon at Rome (the original Attic) – Marble'. Thus reads the entry concerning this piece in Bailey's Inventory of 1837. In this case there seems to be no doubt about the attribution and this capital must be reckoned among the great treasures of Soane's collection of architectural fragments, coming as it does from what is perhaps the most famous of all the classical monuments in Rome, the Pantheon, erected by the Emperor Hadrian between 118 and 128 AD. The stylistic character of the capital is consonant with such a date and provenance. The interior of the Pantheon was redecorated and restuccoed in 1747 by the architect Paolo Posi (1708–76), who replaced a number of pilasters in the upper order of the building, probably because they had been damaged. Six similar capitals are in the British Museum (Townley Collection), one belongs to the Royal Academy and others are in the Museo Profano at Lateran in Rome. Piranesi published a reconstruction of the upper interior of the Pantheon in his *Raccolta de' Tempi Antiche*, 1776, showing one of these capitals. Soane's capital was acquired at the Sir Henry Englefield sale at Christie's on 6th March 1823, lot 84, where it was said to have come 'from the collection of the Duke of St. Albans'.

**Museum number: M821   46.5cm × 52cm**

**Fig. 85**    Silver boat-shaped tureen with a matching oval dish. The makers' mark is that of Peter and Ann Bateman and the date-mark is that for 1795. The tureen is inscribed in Latin, 'Without your help I would not have achieved my fame. Let the iron bridge over the Wear bear witness to this. R. Burdon gave this as a gift to J. Soane, his well-deserving friend'. Rowland Burdon (d.1838), later MP for Sunderland and Chairman of the Hartlepool Dock and Railway Company, first met the young John Soane in Rome in 1778. They travelled extensively together in Italy and Burdon was responsible for taking Soane to Parma where he was elected a member of the Academy. On Soane's return to England in 1780 Burdon gave him one of his first independent commissions – for some rebuilding at his own house, Castle Eden in County Durham. Burdon and Soane remained life-long friends and there are a great many letters from Burdon in the Soane Archive, commenting on European politics, continually urging Soane to visit and in one case commenting on Soane's lectures as published in *The Herald* saying that he 'should like to be your candle-snuffer'.

In 1794 Burdon sought Soane's advice about the possibility of constructing a stone single-span bridge of 236 feet over the River Wear at Sunderland. Soane surveyed the site and expressed doubts. It was eventually decided to drop the idea of a stone bridge and build one of cast iron. This was a great novelty at the time and Soane's support was decisive in the decision to go ahead. At one point John Nash alleged that the idea had been stolen from him by Burdon. The bridge was the great project of Burdon's life and Soane assisted financially when Burdon pledged his own resources to get it built. Soane's enthusiasm for the iron bridge demonstrates his great interest in engineering of an advanced kind. Burdon's commission and gift of this tureen to Soane in 1795 perhaps marked the completion and opening of the bridge.

Burdon continued to consult Soane about the bridge and report regularly on its financial position throughout his life. On 20th May 1835 he wrote 'My Wearmouth bridge has . . . stood its ground most successfully, and though perhaps a little anti-architectural, has justified my engineering, and made me not unworthy of your friendship in a modest degree'. In the last letter he wrote to Soane on 13th August 1836 he recollected their happy days in Italy and reported that the bridge was prospering, adding, 'You my friend were the only person who whispered to me to "go on", which, amongst other acknowledgements, I am now gratified to make'.

**Silver tureen    H (including cover): 35.5cm**

**Fig. 86**  A selection of pieces from a Coalport porcelain dessert service of about 1805–10 produced at the Anstice, Horton and Rose factory. The handles and lobed edges are typical of Coalport and sherds of this pattern have been excavated on the factory site. It is unusual for services of this type to have both ice-pails and tureens and this example was therefore probably to be used either for dinner or dessert. We do not know when or where this colourful service was bought. In Soane's day it was always known as the 'Worcester China' and was kept, along with a large and valuable dinner service of 'India China' (in fact Chinese export porcelain), in the mirrored cupboard at the back of the Shakespeare Recess (see Fig. 99). It seems that Soane regarded these two services as especially valuable – part of his collection of 'works of art' rather than items for ordinary domestic use. The rest of the purely domestic china and glassware was stored in the basement china pantry, conveniently placed next to the kitchen. In a codicil to his Will, dated 22nd August 1836, Soane specified 'the Worcester China and the India China to be kept at the Museum and to be a part thereof'. No other china is mentioned. These two services were therefore listed in George Bailey's Inventory of 1837 along with other works of art, unlike the rest of the domestic china. The Inventory shows that there were then 138 pieces in this service of which only forty-eight now survive. Almost certainly most of it was broken during the 19th century when successive curators lived at the Museum and Soane's domestic china was in every-day use. It was not until the early 1900s, when a Spode and Copeland dinner service was bought for the use of curators, that every-day use of Soane's two prized services of china finally ceased.

**Fig. 87**  Portable pillar barometer, probably by the famous instrument-maker Daniel Quare (1649–1724) of London; early 18th century. Quare produced a considerable number of barometers of this model which he patented. Some, like this one, could either hang on the wall or stand on a table. They are usually made of walnut but a few are of ivory. They vary somewhat in quality. That Soane acquired an antique instrument like this is evidence of his interest in technology (see also Fig. 91), as well as in old furniture of distinction. It certainly formed part of his collection by June 1817 when it is shown in a watercolour of the Breakfast Room.
**Museum number: MP281    H: 100cm**

**Fig. 88**   Jasperware chessmen, modelled in 1783–4 by John Flaxman and manufactured at Josiah Wedgwood's pottery-works at Etruria in Staffordshire. Flaxman's original design-drawing and wax models for some of the figures survive in the Wedgwood Museum at Barlaston. The popularity of chess was increasing at the end of the 18th century and Wedgwood introduced this new line, hoping to sell a great many such sets at 5 guineas each – considerably less than the price asked for the usual ivory or silver sets. In fact, only 130 sets were sold between 1785 and 1795. Flaxman's inspiration for the design of the pieces came from classical, medieval and contemporary sources. The rearing horse on which the knight sits was based on a fragment from the Parthenon frieze which had been brought back to England by Thomas Chandler and belonged to the Society of Dilettanti. Flaxman sought permission to model a copy of it in 1784. Other pieces are clearly inspired by medieval sculpture. Flaxman was a close friend of the poet William Blake, who was serving an apprenticeship with James Basire, the engraver, and working for him on drawings of Gothic monuments in Westminster Abbey in preparation for engraving the plates for Richard Gough's *Sepulchral Monuments* (published in 1796). Some of the chessmen bear a distinct resemblance to figures from medieval tombs drawn for this book and Flaxman may well have had access to the illustrations before publication, through his friendship with Blake. According to tradition Flaxman is supposed to have modelled the Queen on the celebrated actress Sarah Siddons as Lady Macbeth, and the King on her brother, John Phillip Kemble, as Macbeth. When the figures were produced by Wedgwood for sale the bases were often coloured – indeed some sets with figures entirely made of blue jasper were produced in 1790. These particular white jasperware pieces are uncommon and belonged to Flaxman himself. Each figure has the Wedgwood mark and a number on the base. Like most of the items by Flaxman in Soane's collection, these chessmen came to the Museum from Miss Maria Denman, who delivered them to Soane in March 1834. It seems unlikely that Soane used them for playing chess; indeed, there is no complete set in this collection.

**Museum number: X5**

John Soane rebuilt No. 12 in 1792 as a home for himself and his family, and as his place of business. He built an office for himself in the back yard, and the covered passage connecting this to the main house came to be the site of his first display of antiquities, alternating with busts and vases in niches. We hope to re-open this passage in the near future, so as to link the main Museum with the rooms on the ground floor of No. 12, so that the delightful Breakfast Parlour and what was formerly Soane's Dining-Room (which will become a small gallery where changing exhibits are mounted) may once again be seen by the public. In this Link Passage several items of metalwork and some gems will be on display.

**Figs. 89 and 90** A silver calendar watch made by Langley Bradley; 1690s or early 1700s. Bradley was a prominent member of the London Clockmakers' Company, which he joined as an apprentice in 1687, being elected Master from 1726 to 1738. This watch is said to have been the gift of Queen Anne (reigned 1702–14) to Sir Christopher Wren. Langley Bradley made the clock for St Paul's Cathedral in about 1706 so it is not at all inconceivable that he should have made a timepiece to be presented to the architect. The outer case of the watch is of silver with a 24-hour silver dial. Within is a finely worked brass inner case with ornaments in the style of Simon Gribelin (1661–1733) who came to London in about 1680 and was a member of the Clockmakers' Company from 1686, although he worked as an engraver. Gribelin published several books of designs for clock decoration including *Book of severall ornaments* (1682) and *A Book of Ornaments usefull to jewellers, watchmakers and all other Artists* (1697). Around the sides of the inner case are openwork monograms – of Queen Anne – each surmounted by a crown, which mask the inner works. The inner dial of the watch shows the month and is inscribed with the names of the twelve months and their astrological signs. At the time of Soane's death this watch was kept in the Library. Soane would have valued its connection with Wren very highly.

**Museum number: L111    Dia (closed): 6cm**

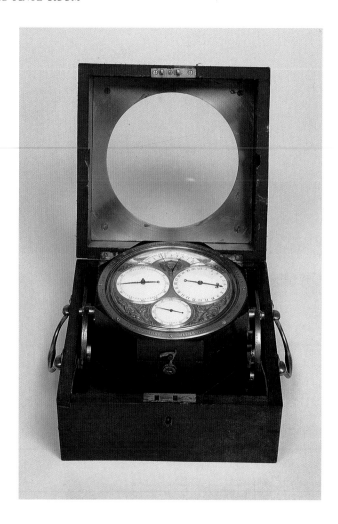

**Fig. 91**    An eight-day marine chronometer by Thomas Mudge (1717–94); late 18th century. Accurate time-keeping at sea is essential to precise navigation. This had long been realised but had been difficult to achieve. In 1714, Parliament passed an Act offering £20,000 to 'such person or persons as shall discover the Longitude'. In 1773 the prize was finally won by John Harrison with his fourth marine time-keeper which can still be seen in the National Maritime Museum at Greenwich. Thomas Mudge subsequently also devised an extremely accurate chronometer, the prototype of which was ready in 1774. His final, third, refined version of 1777 possessed a degree of accuracy not surpassed for nearly a hundred years and Mudge was awarded a prize of £3,000 by the Board of Longitude. Mudge's son, also Thomas, set up a business producing chronometers to his father's design and employing two leading horologists, Howells and Pennington and later, after Howells left the business, Pendleton. Each chronometer was numbered as it was produced and they were sold for between 170 and 180 guineas. Copy No. 2 was dated 1794. Soane's instrument is the tenth copy and is inscribed 'No. 10 – Pennington, Pendleton and Others for the Son of the Inventor'. It is undated but was probably made at Pendleton and Pennington's works in Camberwell. This chronometer is fitted with the original Mudge escapement mechanism and has been recently described as the finest Mudge copy in existence. It seems to have been made for the Duke of Marlborough who paid £167. 10s. for it; a portion of the Marlborough family crest is engraved on the face. It is in near pristine condition and probably never went to sea; it has no gimballs and the box does not appear to be the type made to house a chronometer for marine use. It may well have been intended as a presentation piece.

The main problem with the original Mudge mechanism was that it was extremely complex and required frequent tuning to maintain its accuracy. By the 1790s more commercially viable chronometers were being produced, and Thomas Mudge junior completed only fifteen copies before ceasing business.

Soane's acquisition of this important object reflects his deep interest in technological and scientific matters.

**Museum number: NDR54    15.6cm × 21.4cm × 21.3cm**

**Fig. 92** A plaster figure of Flora after the famous antique marble statue in the Palazzo Farnese in Rome. The 1837 Inventory notes that it is 'coloured to imitate Bronze', although in fact it seems rather to be painted to resemble terracotta. This plaster cast was probably taken from moulds in turn taken from a terracotta figure loosely based on the Farnese Flora by the sculptor John Michael Rysbrack in 1759. Rysbrack's figure was made to grace a room at Teddesley, a house being built and furnished at that time by Sir Edward Littleton. The sculptor also produced a full-sized version in marble for Henry Hoare at Stourhead. The porcelain factory at Bow, in London's East End, produced a figure after this model and it seems quite probable that the moulds from which the factory's porcelain figures were cast were also used for making figures in plaster like this one. A figure of Flora based on Rysbrack's model was also produced in Coade Stone in the 1770s.
**Museum number: A64    H: 52cm**

**Fig. 93** A late 17th-century key described in the 1837 Inventory of Works of Art as 'richly embossed and gilded with a cipher surmounted by a crown, supposed to have been the key of some of the Royal Apartments at Windsor Castle. This key was formerly in the possession of Mr. George Davis, locksmith of Windsor who held the appointment of locksmith to the Castle for many years having succeeded his father therein who had previously held the same appointment for a long period.' However, in the 1950s the key was identified as the gold key to the State Rooms built by Sir Christopher Wren at Hampton Court Palace. The cipher on the ornate bow is that of William III and Queen Mary combined. Recent investigation has shown that although a facsimile of the first Earl of Portland's key for the State Apartments at Hampton Court with an identical cipher survives, it has a different stem and lock to Soane's key – and no other surviving royal keys match this one. In his capacity as Architect attached to the Office of Works Soane was involved in general survey work at Hampton Court. He certainly knew George Davis, who was paid £16. 18s. and £13. 14s. in May and September 1825, apparently for locks at 13 Lincoln's Inn Fields although it is possible that part of these payments was for this by then ancient key. It is at any rate a very handsome specimen of the locksmith's art of the late 17th century.
**Museum number: L113    Length: 13.5cm**

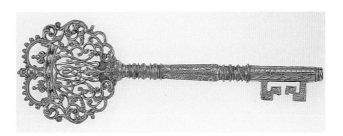

**Fig. 94**    View of the Breakfast Parlour at No. 12 Lincoln's Inn Fields, Soane's first house in the square, drawn by Joseph Gandy in November 1798. Built in 1792, the room served as an informal dining-room and as a library, there being six mahogany bookcases along the walls. The informal character of the room is indicated by the presence of simulated bamboo chairs – always associated with light-hearted settings – and by the charming pergola-like decoration of the ceiling which was painted by John Crace in 1793–4. In the background is a handsome library desk which must have been designed by Soane and appears to be that now standing against the pier at the south end of the Library in No. 13 (see Fig. 7). In front is a reading-stand and nearby is a sofa, above which hangs a convex mirror. Hanging above the bookcases are five Piranesi engravings and (centre, right) Soane's drawing of the Banqueting House, Whitehall, which won him the Royal Academy Silver Medal in 1772. Many of the smaller items in the room, together with two of the bookcases, survive and it is the intention to restore the room to its 1790s appearance. The painted ceiling has already been revealed from under some fifteen layers of white distemper. Ceilings painted to resemble a pergola like this were much in favour in 16th-century Italy and came into fashion again in the 1780s and 1790s all over Europe. Here the painting is applied to the earliest of Soane's 'star-fish' ceilings – a form he often used later. Its origin seems to lie in drawings of the ceiling designs of Etruscan tombs in Bartoli's *Gli Antichi Sepolchri*, 1768. Curiously out of scale are the figures of John Soane and his wife Elizabeth, together with their sons John and George who would respectively have been twelve and eleven years old when Gandy executed this drawing.

**Drawing 14.6.1    645mm × 650mm**

# THE BREAKFAST PARLOUR
## NO. 13

**Fig. 95**  The Breakfast Parlour at No. 13 Lincoln's Inn Fields as it looked in November 1825, one of several views of the room included in the volume of watercolour views of Soane's house and of objects on show in it at that time. It is possible to see how accurately the room has been portrayed by referring to the next illustration which shows the room today from much the same viewpoint. Most of the features remain untouched although Soane made numerous minor changes to this famous room after 1825. The principal of these was the filling with convex mirrors of the four apertures in the flattened dome, the addition of moveable planes on either side of the window, and the fitting of numerous small convex mirrors as punctuating ornaments. The chandelier to be seen in the photograph is not old. If the room has lost anything, it is its colourfulness but some measure of this is about to be restored when coloured glass is again installed in the skylights. Of the two double doors opening into the Dome area (on the left), the right-hand inner door is closed to reveal its mirror-glass facing. The doors opposite (i.e. closest to the viewer) are similarly faced. The central window over the desk (which has a pull-out seat) looks on to the Monument Court, where the Pasticcio can just be seen, reaching up from the basement level (see Fig. 24). The deep window on the right looks over to the window of Soane's Study where the small upright Venetian blinds are visible (see Fig. 15) as is the skylight filled with alternating dark and pale yellow glass.
**Sketches and Drawing Volume (Vol. 82), p.26**
**185mm × 246mm**

**Fig. 96**    The ceiling and north wall of the Breakfast Parlour in 1990. The central picture of the north wall is a large watercolour of Mrs. Soane's tomb (see Fig. 3). In front stands a winged figure of Victory which was placed in that position by Soane ten days before he died on 20th January, 1837. He saw the juxtaposition of these two works of art as symbolic of a triumph over Death. The figure was made by Flaxman after an antique statue he had seen in Rome which is now in the museum at Kassel. Visible in this view are six coloured engravings showing part of a scheme of mural decoration discovered in 1777 in the ruins of a classical building in the grounds of the Villa Negroni, on the Esquiline Hill, Rome. This discovery caused great excitement and within a year an architect named Camillo Buti had drawn and published a plate of the building and had announced his intention of publishing thirteen plates showing the wall-paintings. Buti engaged the celebrated painter Anton Raphael Mengs to copy the paintings, a task which he began in spite of his failing health and 'the dampness of the deep place in which they stood'. Mengs only produced three of the thirteen drawings before he died, after which the project was taken up by his brother-in-law, Anton von Maron. The drawings were engraved by Angelo

Campanella and the first three appeared in 1778; the twelfth only came out in 1802. The planned thirteenth drawing does not seem to have been executed. Soane owned Plates I–XII and further copies of four of them. He had eight of them framed and hung on the walls of his Breakfast Parlour at No. 13.

These engravings no doubt inspired Soane's treatment of the decoration of the adjacent Library–Dining-Room. Copies of the same engravings were used for mural decoration in a closet in the Castle of Lançut in Poland. Some of the actual paintings were bought by Lord Hervey, the mercurial Bishop of Derry (see Fig. 10), soon after their discovery. He intended to use them to adorn his seaside house, Downhill, in Ireland, but there is no evidence that they ever reached that destination. The murals, however, evidently influenced the decoration of the Pompeian room at the Bishop's English country residence at Ickworth in Suffolk. Buti was concerned that the copies of these paintings should be rendered 'with the most scrupulous exactness . . . so that one can form an idea of the taste of the ancients in this type of mixed ornamental and figural painting'. The original building apparently dated from about 134 AD and the engravings form an important record of the appearance of an elegant late Hadrianic villa in Rome.

Fig. 97    Sir John Soane's dog, Fanny, 'the faithful companion, the delight the solace of his leisure hours', painted by James Ward, RA in 1822. Fanny had been Mrs. Soane's pet dog and is shown on her lap in a posthumous portrait by Jackson to be seen in the Picture Room. There are two portraits of Fanny in the Breakfast Parlour, one by Van Assen and this present small painting by the leading British animal painter of the time. Soane paid £42 for this picture which was painted two years after Fanny's death. The architectural setting in which Ward has placed his subject, complete with a distant view of the Erechtheion (in Athens), is especially charming. Fanny died at midnight on Christmas Day 1820 and on the following Wednesday, the 27th, Soane wrote in his *Notebook*, 'Fanny buried in the monument prepared for her in the Courtyard at 7 o'clock in the morning: Alas, poor Fanny! faithful, affectionate, disinterested friend, Farewell!' The Courtyard in this context meant the front yard of No. 13. Fanny's remains are now contained in the stone structure at the head of the 'Monk's Tomb' in the Yard outside the Monk's Parlour, which was erected in 1824, and bears the inscription 'Alas poor Fanny'.

**Museum number: P189 (BR)    24.4cm × 19.7cm**

Fig. 98    Plaster cast of the 'Chellini Madonna' by Donatello. The original bronze, now one of the prized possessions of the Victoria and Albert Museum, was given by Donatello to the distinguished Florentine physician Giovanni Chellini (1372/3–1462) in return for medical treatment in the year 1456. Chellini recorded that this small roundel was 'hollowed out' on the back 'so that melted glass could be cast on to it and it would make the same figures as those on the other side' (i.e. on the face). In fact the original is remarkable in that the reverse is an exact negative replica of the front, which is said to be a unique phenomenon in the history of sculpture, and it is interesting that the image on the back was intended for making casts in glass. Donatello seems to have been interested in the problems of making figures in low relief in coloured glass and it is sad to think that Soane, who was himself so fascinated by coloured glass and installed it in many of his buildings (including his own house), cannot have known what the great sculptor had had in mind nearly four centuries before he acquired this cast in plaster and put it on the wall of his Breakfast Parlour where it has hung ever since. However, he knew it was 'after a work by Donatello' (1835 *Description*). It is not known when the bronze came to England but it was in the collection of the Marquis of Rockingham (d.1782) at Wentworth Woodhouse and subsequently passed to his nephew, the fourth Earl Fitzwilliam. The cast was almost certainly made after the bronze arrived in this country; it came into the possession of the painter Henry Howard, RA (1769–1847) who presented it to Soane, his patron, sometime between 1832 and 1835.

**Museum number: BR30    Dia: 23cm**

# THE SHAKESPEARE RECESS

**Fig. 99**    Plaster cast of a bust of William Shakespeare, inscribed on the back 'Moulded by Geo: Bullock from the origenal [sic] in the church at Stratford, Decr. 1814'. George Bullock (1778–1818) began his career as a sculptor but later established an important furnishing and cabinetmaking business, first in Liverpool and then in London. For a short while, from April 1809, he was in partnership in Liverpool with Joseph Gandy (see Fig. 31), who had previously worked for Soane and in whose office John Soane junior was at the time a trainee. It was the antiquarian John Britton (see Fig. 48) who prevailed upon Bullock to make a mould from the Shakespeare monument at Stratford-upon-Avon in 1814. The exercise took longer than Bullock had anticipated but he wrote to Britton that he was pleased to give up the time from 'my London affairs' because he believed the bust to be an extremely good likeness of the Bard, having perceived 'evident signs of its being taken from a cast', by which he presumably meant a life or death mask. Like many of their contemporaries Bullock and Britton had a great interest in Shakespeare's physiognomy and Bullock even invited Dr. J. C. Spurzheim,

one of the founders of the theory of phrenology, to view the bust over breakfast shortly after his return from Stratford. In 1816 Britton published a pamphlet, a copy of which is in Soane's Library, entitled *Remarks on the Monumental Bust of Shakespeare at Stratford-upon-Avon*, defending the likeness.

Soane owned two other busts of Shakespeare (including one by Bullock, reduced in scale), and some twenty paintings and drawings of Shakespearian subjects. In addition he acquired copies of the first three folio editions of Shakespeare's works published in 1623, 1632 and 1664. This bust was placed by Soane in the Shakespeare Recess, a niche off the staircase intended as a shrine to the Bard, whom Soane evidently revered. It was cleaned in 1990 and repainted its original colour – a pale stone colour very different from the sombre shade which it had acquired and that may be seen here. Almost all the plaster casts in the Museum have been painted, in not a few cases many times, and are now mostly much darker than they would have been in Soane's day.

**Museum number: SC18**    60cm × 36.5cm × 80cm

**Fig. 100**   This handsome composition, which hangs in the Loggia, is inscribed 'Drawing by Sir P.P. Rubens – Design for an Emblematical Frame for a Portrait of King Charles I'. On the left are the figures of the Three Graces and below the globe, a rudder of state and a scythe. On the right is the figure of Justice shown without a blindfold and with her scales awry. If this symbolism refers to the martyrdom of Charles I, who was executed in 1649, then this design cannot be by Rubens himself, as he died in 1640. Modern scholarship ascribes it to Theodoor van Thulden (1607–76) who was a pupil and subsequently an assistant of Rubens. This drawing is identical in composition to another by Van Thulden in the National Gallery of Scotland, Edinburgh, which is incised for engraving and blackened on the back for transfer. However, an extensive search has not brought to light any published engraving of Charles I framed in this way. Two collectors' marks can be seen on the drawing; PIL for Lankrink and R for Jonathan Richardson senior (see Fig. 40). It is not known when or where Soane acquired it but he thought it was by Rubens and was very proud of it.

**Museum number: P236 (SDR)**    470mm × 445mm

**Fig. 101** A birds-eye perspective of the Bank of England executed by Joseph Michael Gandy in 1830. Although often referred to as 'the Bank in ruins', this representation is in fact a cut-away perspective by means of which the principal interior features may be shown. A view of the Rotunda at the Bank, actually shown as a ruin, may be seen in the Picture Room. Soane began building at the Bank in 1792 and the present drawing records his achievements on the completion of his work in 1830. This drawing was exhibited at the Royal Academy in that year and has always hung within the planes in the North Drawing-Room; luckily it was shown on the inside face so was not ravaged by constant, unrelenting exposure to daylight as has been the fate of those drawings still shown on the outer faces (nothing can be done to reverse this damage so they have been left in their original positions). **Museum number: P267 (NDR)** 725mm × 1,290mm

**Fig. 102**    Design by George Dance the Younger (1741–1825) for a chimneypiece and mural decoration in the Egyptian taste, for the Great Library at Lansdowne House in Berkeley Square where Dance was working between 1788 and 1791. The head of Athena to be seen here was exchanged for a more appropriate Egyptian bust when the scheme was executed. The design of the chimneypiece was inspired by plates in Piranesi's *Diverse Maniere*. The chimneypiece was removed in 1935. John Soane was apprenticed to Dance at the age of fifteen in 1768 and remained a close friend of his former master until the latter's death in 1825. In 1836 he paid Sir Charles Dance, the architect's son, £500 for the cabinet containing a large collection of Dance's drawings including this specimen which shows admirably Dance's delicate touch and nice sense of colour. The cabinet, on a black-painted and embellished base probably designed by Soane to make it seem shrine-like, first stood in the Monk's Parlour but was later moved upstairs to the North Drawing-Room so that the drawings could be close to the rest of Soane's large collection of architectural drawings. **Dance 3.3.2    335mm × 500mm**

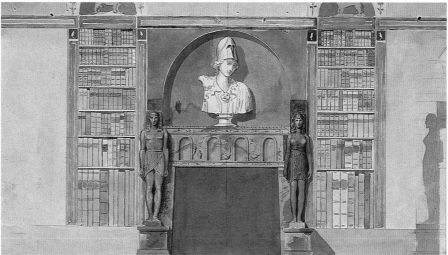

**Fig. 103** Another charming drawing by George Dance, also from the Dance Cabinet, showing a plan and sectional elevation of an oval dining-room. Appropriate ornament for a dining-room – trailing vines with grapes – may be seen on the walls and on the cove of the ceiling. In the apse-like recess stands the sideboard decked with plate. The room is lit by a large rose window over the entrance door and by an oculus in the domed roof. Dance's ingenious handling of light was to have a profound effect on Soane. Dance was not only an architect; he was also an artist noted for his portrait studies which he regularly exhibited at the Royal Academy. Consequently his architectural drawings are often enlivened by figures like those of the diners seen here. This intriguing unidentified design has much in common with Dance's design for the Library at Lansdowne House, 1788–91 (see also Fig. 102).

**Dance 3.13.11    190mm × 235mm**

**Fig. 104**    *Opposite*: Detail from Turner's oil-painting of 'Van Tromp's barge entering the Texel in 1645', which was exhibited at the Royal Academy in 1831 and for which Soane apparently paid £262. 10s. in that year. In Soane's own *Description* of his house in 1835 he claims that this 'fine picture by Turner is always reckoned among the chefs d'oeuvre of that great artist'. The original frame which still surrounds the picture is a splendid expression of the rococo-revival style that was in fashion during the second quarter of the 19th century.

Maarten Harpentzoon van Tromp (1597–1653) was one of the most dashing naval commanders of the 17th century, though why Turner should have chosen to paint at least four pictures of van Tromp subjects is not obvious. As a child van Tromp was captured by the English and made to serve for two years as a cabin-boy. This no doubt made him familiar with English ways which may have helped him in his early encounters with the Royal Navy. It is not known whether there is any substance in the story that he had a broom tied to his masthead to show how he had swept the English from the seas but he was eventually defeated and, indeed, was killed in a battle with the English fleet off the Dutch coast.

**Museum number: P272 (NDR)    90cm × 122cm**

**Fig. 105**   One of a pair of candleholders; English, about 1800. One might at first glance think these charming figures were French bronzes but they are in fact made of plaster and painted black. Such ornaments must have been fairly common in middle-class settings like Soane's house but their fragile nature has ensured that few examples survive. The figure which was the inspiration for these two, entitled *L'Etude*, has no candle nozzle and both hands support a book. It was by Louis Simon Boizot who from 1773 until 1809 was the Director of Sculpture at the Sèvres porcelain factory near Paris. The figure, introduced in the early 1780s in hard-paste porcelain, was then reproduced in bronze and incorporated in a wide variety of decorative ornaments. This figure, with its pair, originally stood on the chimneypiece in the Dining-Room (see Fig. 2).

**Museum number: B1**
**20cm × 24.5cm**

**Fig. 106**   Bronze figure of Mercury after Giovanni da Bologna (Giambologna; 1529–1608). Soane believed this to be by the master himself, a small version of the famous figure today in the Museo Nazionale in Florence (The Bargello) which was cast in 1564. The figure was so popular that numerous copies and versions were subsequently produced. Metallurgical analysis has indicated that this particular figure could well have been executed by one of Giambologna's assistants in the late 16th or early 17th century. The artist most likely to have been responsible is Pietro Tacca (1557–1640) who entered the master's service in 1592 (see also Fig. 82). The figure itself is handsome but the mask on which it stands is a fine work in its own right. This sculpture was given to Soane sometime between 1824 and 1830 by his old friend Alexander Day, the painter (1772–1841), who had purchased it at the Mark Sykes sale at Christie's on 14th May 1824, where it was recorded as having been 'purchased from the Ricardi Palace' which presumably means the Palazzo Medici-Riccardi in Florence. If true, the figure has an impressive provenance. It can be seen in Fig. 15 standing on the chimneypiece in the Study in 1825.

**Museum number: SC20    H: 70cm**

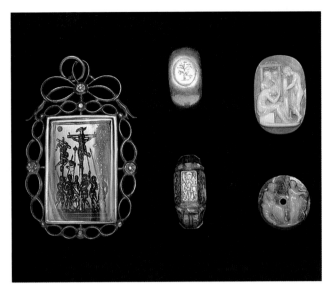

Soane bought a collection of 275 gemstones from the first Duke of Buckingham and Chandos in about 1834 for £1,000. About half of them came from the Braschi Collection in Rome and the rest had been assembled by the Archbishop of Tarentum. Monsignor Capece-Latro was a prominent churchman and had been a Minister in the Neapolitan Government when Naples was under Napoleonic rule. On his retirement he devoted himself to collecting and entertaining distinguished foreign visitors including, presumably, the Duke of Buckingham who probably acquired gems from the Archbishop in 1828–9. Some of the stones were antique but a number were in fact quite new when Soane acquired them, although he did not know this. Many talented Italian artists turned to cutting semi-precious stones in the absence of commissions for large-scale works during the neoclassical period and many of their works are scarcely distinguishable from antique gems. Many were produced as deliberate fakes, often with false provenances. Soane had two special showcases, lined with white silk, made for his collection of gems, and they were displayed in the North Drawing-Room.

**Fig. 107** With the exception of the top central stone (from the Capece-Latro collection), this small selection comes from the Braschi Collection. *Left to right, top*: a neoclassical white onyx idealised portrait cameo against a chalcedony background with a pierced silver-gilt pendant setting. This gem, like all the other neoclassical gems photographed here, was thought by Soane to be antique: a Renaissance cameo of carnelian and breccia, with a Bacchic procession based on an antique model: a neoclassical cameo of glass paste imitating sardonyx with a portrait of Minerva. *Below, left to right*: an antique cameo of sardonyx bearing a portrait of the Emperor

Vespasian (69–79 AD): an antique sardonyx and breccia cameo of a lion: a cameo of sardonyx showing St George and the Dragon, almost certainly made by Benedetto Pistrucci (1784–1855) but sold as antique in Rome. Pistrucci began gem-engraving aged fourteen in Rome and in his first year of work cut a cameo which passed into the Cabinet of the Empress of Russia as antique. He later produced gems for many dealers, including one named Bonelli, notorious for passing off newly cut gems as antique originals. In 1815 Pistrucci came to England and soon met Wellesley Pole, the Master of the Mint. This resulted in a St George and the Dragon by Pistrucci, very like Soane's gem, appearing in 1817 on the reverse of the new gold half-sovereign. The same figure is still used on the reverse of sovereigns, which are held in the Bank of England. Pistrucci remained in England until his death so he could have seen his own gem on display in Soane's collection masquerading as a valuable antique cameo.

**Fig. 108** Further specimens from the Braschi Collection. *Left*: Italian 16th-century onyx intaglio of the Crucifixion. *Top centre*: a Moorish gold ring said to have been found in a tomb at Granada (Spain). *Bottom centre*: a medieval gilt brass ring bearing the image of St Barbara, possibly a betrothal ring. St Barbara was very commonly depicted on such rings because of the belief that she protected against sudden death. *Top right*: a neoclassical white onyx cameo on chalcedony depicting Achilles mourning the death of Patroclus – a copy of a famed antique gem known as 'The Tears of Achilles' (now in the Lewes House collection). *Bottom right*: a cameo of sardonyx of uncertain date (likely to be Renaissance) depicting Aesculapaius and Hygeia.

**Figs. 109 and 110**    Medals struck to celebrate people of note, victories and other important events during the Consular and Imperial reign of Napoleon Bonaparte, 1799–1815. Such medals were produced in large numbers at the Paris Mint, usually in gold, silver and copper or bronze. Initially, many of them were of indifferent execution and design but after 1802 under the direction of the famous antiquarian, Baron Vivant Denon, some of the best French sculptors of the period worked for the Mint, applying their talents to medal design. The series of 140 Napoleon Medals in the Soane Museum is not complete but is said to have been selected by Denon for the Empress Joséphine herself who, although divorced and set aside by the Emperor, was still devoted to him. Indeed, in Soane's own description of the medals it is claimed of Joséphine that 'where the record of her husband thus given was connected with circumstances in her own opinion indicative of blame, . . . [she] withdrew them from the rest, anxious to preserve unalloyed the glory she adored and the greatness she had shared'. According to a pencil note at the back of a printed catalogue of Napoleon Medals, which is in the collection, Soane's medals were put into a case by 'the Emperor of Russia with Sir Francis Chantrey'. Whether true or not, Tsar Alexander did visit London in June 1814 and summoned Soane to meet him at the Bank of England on the 19th. Soane presented the Emperor with drawings of the Bank and the Emperor gave Soane a diamond ring. The Napoleon

medals were certainly in Soane's possession by 1830; in 1834 they were placed in two cases in the South Drawing-Room Loggia. **Museum numbers: SDR 20 and SDR 21; 1–140**

**Fig. 109**    Two medals struck at the Paris Mint in 1804 showing views in the Louvre Museum in Paris. The left hand one shows the 'Salle de l'Apollon' with the Apollo Belvedere in pride of place in the centre while that on the right depicts the Salle du Laocöon (the old entrance hall to the Museum) with the antique marble Laocöon group at the far end. Both medals are by Bertrand Andrieu. Both have on the reverse a head of Napoleon crowned with a laurel wreath – in imitation of the coins of Imperial Rome.

The Musée de la Republique in the Palais du Louvre was opened in 1793 showing works of art confiscated from royal and aristocratic collections during the Revolution. In the 1790s, the Museum also came to house works looted from Belgium, Germany and Italy under Napoleon and thus a symbol of France's military might. It was later renamed the Musée Napoleon. The French justified their seizures on the grounds that France, as the land of Liberty and Equality, was the proper home for all works of genius. Joseph Lebreton wrote during the Italian Campaign, 'The French Republic, because of its strength and the superiority of its civilisation and artists, is the only country on earth that can offer these masterpieces an inviolable asylum', while the Louvre

administration in 1795 declared that 'Victory has wrested these monuments from the degrading gaze of slaves . . . and delivered them to the pure and brilliant light of day, where they belong'. Great trouble was taken in the care of the statues and in their restoration after they arrived in Paris. The transfer of the Italian items culminated in a triumphal entry into Paris and a public festival on the 27th July 1798. The Apollo Belvedere reached Paris in this procession carried in a garlanded case and was then put on display (as shown here) in the Musée Napoleon. Soane almost certainly saw both the Apollo and the Laocöon during his visit to Paris in August 1814. After the overthrow of Napoleon in 1815 the French government was obliged to return some five thousand works of art to their former owners and the Apollo and Laocöon were among those returned to the Vatican.
**Dia of both medals: 35mm**

**Fig. 110** More medals produced at the Paris Mint under the direction of Vivant Denon whose name, along with that of the designer, appears on all five.

*Top left*: designed by Brenet and one of two struck to commemorate the Battle of Friedland, a decisive victory over the Russians in Poland, won on 14th June 1807, the anniversary of the Battle of Marengo in 1800. On the reverse of the medal is a laurel-crowned head of Napoleon by Andrieu. *Top centre*: designed by Gayrard showing Napoleon

in profile (as Roman emperors were shown on coins) wearing his general's uniform. The reverse shows a figure of Victory hovering above the earth – on which Italy and Greece are visible. This commemorates the Battle of Montenotte, the first victory of the Italian Campaign, 11th April 1796. *Top right* is a medal struck in 1810 and designed by Depaulis. It commemorates the setting up, by a decree of 29th March 1809, of an establishment for female orphans of members of the Legion of Honour, at Écouen and St Denis. The basket shown on the right contains various emblems of female education. *Below left* is a medal by Jeuffroy marking the Battle of Moscow, 7th September 1812, when the French were still victorious and before the celebrated retreat of the following winter. *Below right* is a medal of 1807 by Brenet. Across the bottom is inscribed OTTO III. BOLESLAU. A. MI. NEAPOLIO FRIDERICO AUG. A. MDCCCVII (Otto III to Boleslau in 1001. Napoleon to Frederic Augustus in 1807). Napoleon was calling himself Emperor and pretended to have succeeded to all the rights of the Holy Roman Emperors in the West. The mention of the events of the year 1001 was intended to remind the Poles of their ancient obligations to the Emperors at a time when Napoleon had recently set up a puppet Grand-Duchy of Warsaw under the Treaties of Tilsit in 1807.
**Dia of all medals: 40mm**

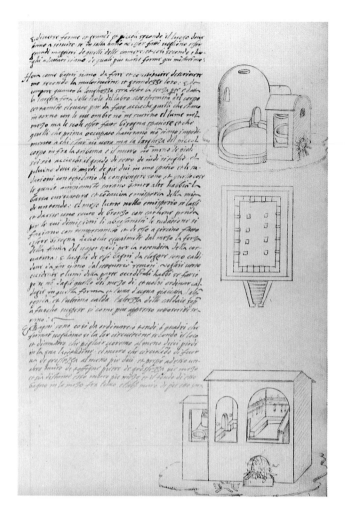

The major part of Sir John Soane's collection of drawings, books and manuscripts is now housed in the Research Library, adjoining the South Drawing-Room.

**Fig. 111**    A page from an important architectural treatise written in about 1480 by the great architect Francesco di Giorgio Martini (1439–1501). The original manuscript is in the Laurentian Library in Florence (Codex Ashburnham 361) but the Soane Museum's manuscript copy must date from about 1540 and was probably executed in Siena, Francesco's native city, or possibly in Venice. At some point it was in the Biblioteca Soranzo in Venice but it is not known how Soane came to possess this precious volume, with its fine hand and delightful illustrations. Soane's copy, which is in fact now rather more complete than the original, bears a bookseller's inscription describing the contents as a 'Treatise on Fortifications, Architecture, Machines in Italian with numerous drawings very neatly executed with the pen'. The page reproduced here shows sketches of a bathroom and 'sweating closet' (what we now call a *sauna*). The latter had underfloor heating and double-skinned walls to conduct the heat. Note the bath towels hanging on the pegs.
**Volume 118, p. 41    Paper size 353mm × 245mm**

**Fig. 112**    Pages in a volume of designs known as 'The Vasari Album' and undoubtedly associated with Giorgio Vasari (1512–74). Some may be in his hand; others are probably the work of assistants. Whether the drawings are primarily from the drawing office, headed by Vasari, which served the arch-ducal court of the Medici at Florence, is not yet clear. There are many designs for church ornament, and the designs may spring from an even wider background. Among the drawings are designs for fireworks, trophies, and (it seems) theatre scenery. Many are for grotesque ornament and may be by an assistant of Vasari, Marchetti da Faenza (d.1588) who was particularly skilful in handling this idiom. Shown here is the design for a wine-fountain surmounted by a horse-finial with a shield bearing the Medici arms. The tripod stands are for wash basins.
**Volume 132, f.9.    345mm × 237mm**

**Fig. 113**  This would seem to be a design for a piece of furniture. It comes from a pattern-book containing designs, all seemingly by the same hand, that are certainly north Italian and probably date from the late 15th century (they are executed on vellum). The sketches seem to be a record of things seen by a designer of ornament, noted down for future reference as a source of inspiration. Assuming that the dark rectangles represent drawers and that the top two drawers could not be above eye-level for practical reasons, this elaborate piece of furniture, if that is what it is, would have been about six feet high (180 cm). There may have been a pair of drawers in the base as well. It was evidently to be decorated with a good deal of carved ornament; some of the panels seem to be decorated with inlay while the drawer-fronts seem to rely on richly veined 'veneers' for their effect. Among the other designs in this important volume are proposals for thrones, panelling, perspective *lavoro di intarsio* and other woodwork, as well as designs which must have been intended for metalwork (parade helmets, showy vessels probably for displaying on a *credenza*, and salt-cellars), and friezes, cornices, and a chimneypiece. The original owner of this pattern-book may have been a designer of the second rank, working under an artist of greater stature at a court like that of Ferrara, ready to provide designs for a wide range of items at the behest of the local ruler.

**North Italian Sketchbook (Vol. 122), f. 29**
**312mm × 214mm**

**Fig. 114**    Drawing by an Italian artist of the 18th century (possibly Giuseppe Manocchi, *c.*1731–82) of grotesque decoration at the Vatican; one of twelve such drawings in a volume acquired by Soane for £3. 4*s.* at George Garrett's sale in 1833 when they were described as 'A Collection of Drawings of the Ornaments of the Vatican etc. highly finished in colours, red morocco'. Some similar drawings, by the same hand, are among the Adam drawings in Soane's collection. These two groups of drawings are a reminder that foreign architects studying in Rome in the 18th century could draw inspiration not only from ruined antique classical monuments but also from the work of Italian contemporaries who were of course familiar with the decoration produced during each stage of their city's history including the *grottesche* of the Renaissance and the *arabesques* of early neoclassicism. This drawing reflects an awareness of both these styles.
**Volume 130, f.2    123mm × 365mm**

**Fig. 115**    *Opposite left*: Design for a jewel-cabinet, almost certainly by François Joseph Belanger (1744–1818) who, in 1769, provided the design for a larger jewel-cabinet for the marriage of Marie Antoinette, the future Queen of France. At that time she was still Dauphine, and the cabinet of the present design must presumably be a pendant to hers since it bears the initials L.D. that must therefore stand for 'Louis, Dauphin'. Although the legs are different, many of the ornamental features of the two designs are similar, and the dolphins topping the crowns are very evident on both. At present we have no knowledge of a pendant cabinet, or pair of cabinets, but a combing of the archives of the *Menus Plaisirs*, the organisation that supplied the French Crown with occasional furnishings of all kinds and of which Belanger was appointed *dessinateur* in 1767, might well reveal further information about this design, which at any rate must be for an important royal French commission. The Soane's drawing is in a small volume containing various architectural and ornamental drawings by unidentified French draughtsmen. The significance of this particular design was only established during the preparation of the present book. The Marie Antoinette cabinet was made by the cabinetmaker M.B. Evald assisted by the carver Augustin Bocciardi. Jacques Philippe Houdon, brother of the famous sculptor, provided the model for an important mount which was then cast in bronze and gilded by Gouthiere. The design for this costly piece of furniture is in the Bibliothèque Nationale in Paris. It is an early expression of neoclassicism.
**Volume 6 (A.L.46.A.), f.44    193mm × 135mm**

**Fig. 116** *Above right*: Design for the chimneypiece in the dining-room at Spencer House, London, by John Vardy (d.1765), dated 1755. This important building on the edge of Green Park was designed by Vardy and built between 1756 and 1765 in a late version of the English neo-Palladian style. The main rooms on the *piano nobile*, however, were designed by James 'Athenian' Stuart (1713–88). They are a very early expression of the neo-Grecque style, arising from his study of Classical Greek architecture, which led to the publication in 1762 of his book, *The Antiquities of Athens*, with Nicholas Revett. Stuart and Revett's tour, and the subsequent publication of their book, was sponsored by the Society of Dilettanti and it is often claimed that the Society, who regarded themselves as arbiters of taste in such matters, wanted to persuade the young Lord Spencer (himself a member of the Society) to adopt Athenian Stuart's style in preference to earlier forms of classicism. However, the fact that Colonel George Gray, the Society's influential secretary, signed this drawing on the back, noting that he had approved 'the lower part', shows that members of the Society felt qualified to judge all variants of the classical style and probably did not see the distinction between Vardy's style and that of Stuart in quite such clear-cut terms as we like to think are so apparent today. The chimneypiece was executed without the rejected overmantel shown here but was removed from Spencer House during the Second World War and installed at Althorp, the Spencer family seat in Northamptonshire, where it remains today. A replica of this chimneypiece was recently installed at Spencer House.
**Drawing, 69.1.1    473mm × 282mm**

**Fig. 117** *Previous pages*: Unexecuted design by Sir William Chambers (1723–96) for a mausoleum for Frederick, Prince of Wales, to be built in Kew Gardens, Surrey, dated 1751. This fine ink and watercolour drawing is the first known design by an English architect to be represented in perspective in a realistic landscape setting with naturalistic lighting effects. The Prince of Wales died in March 1751 and it is likely that Chambers was asked to supply designs for a mausoleum by the Dowager Princess Augusta, whom he had met at Kew in 1749. Chambers, then in his late twenties, executed this drawing in Rome where he was strongly influenced by the neoclassical ideas of several young French architects and designers, such as Le Geauy and Le Lorrain, who were stipendiaries of the French Academy there. The pictorial presentation of this design owes much to their dramatic perspectives produced each year for masquerades at the Chinea Festival. It is composed in the spirit of a classical Roman monument; its scale was to have been vast, as the figures in the foreground show. Soane may well have acquired this important drawing from the Chambers sale at Christie's on 6th June 1811.
**Drawing 17.7.11    490mm × 700mm**

**Fig. 118**    A charming watercolour described in the 1837 Inventory as 'A Garden scene with specimens of various kinds of trees', by George Barret the Elder, RA (1732–78), signed with his monogram in the bottom left-hand corner. Barret was an Irish landscape painter who was one of the forty founder Academicians of the Royal Academy in December 1768. Soane was closely associated with the Academy throughout his long career and consequently it is not surprising that he had three of Barret's works in his Museum – this drawing, a self-portrait (bought in 1798 after Barret's death) and a 'View in Mr. Lock's Park at Leatherhead', which hangs in the Picture Room. Bryan's *Dictionary*, 1816, provides an appropriate contemporary comment on Barret's watercolours: 'His colouring is excellent and there is a freshness and dewy brightness in his verdure which is only to be met with in English scenery, and which he has perfectly represented'.
**Drawing, 69.3.1    340mm × 460mm**

**Fig. 119**    Aquatint view of the 'Hôtel de Madame la Marquise du Brunoy', close to the Champs-Elysées in Paris. Probably made during the 1780s, just prior to the outbreak of the French Revolution. This is one of a series of coloured views of Paris produced by the Le Campion brothers which are mounted in a leather-bound album on blue paper, along with a series of monochrome engravings by Vallardi. Into the front of the volume is pasted Vallardi's bookseller's card, so it is possible that the prints were purchased from his shop in the Boulevard Poissonnière, Paris. They were probably sold loose and the purchaser must have pasted them into this album and slipped in the relevant pages from his notebook giving a commentary on the buildings and their occupants. The notes are written in French and the style indicates that they were written by a Frenchman – they are certainly not by Soane – and their content is more anecdotal than architectural. Soane may have purchased this volume on 7th September 1814 when there is a bill paid to Boydell and Company for a book entitled 'Monumens de Paris'. This was just two days after Soane's return from a twenty-one-day trip to Paris – taking advantage of the peace that followed the first capture of Napoleon, before his escape from Elba.
**Architectural Library**, 23.C    190 mm × 147mm

**Fig. 120**  Red chalk drawing by Charles Percier (1764–1838). On this fanciful composition of Roman antique fragments Percier has written an indication of the source of each motif (*Monte Cavallo/Foro Traiano/Albano*). The Museum catalogue suggests this drawing was executed in about 1802 but at that point Percier (with P.F.L. Fontaine) was busy working on a host of projects for Napoleon Bonaparte and his wife Joséphine. He was actually in Rome between 1786 and 1791 and it seems more likely that this sketch was made during that highly productive study-tour (see Fig. 11). The drawing was presented by Percier to the sculptor John Flaxman when the latter was in Paris in 1802. Flaxman's sister-in-law, Maria Denman, gave it to Soane on his eighty-first birthday in September 1834.

**Drawing 48.5.5  310mm × 195mm**

**Fig. 121**   The Library contains books covering a very wide range of subjects that could be of interest to architects – from essays on how to prevent chimneys from smoking, to drainage, bricklaying and surveying. It is also a fruitful source of information on interior decoration, as this reproduction of one half of a double-plate illustration in a French folio volume shows. The work is a presentation volume commemorating the celebrations held by the City of Paris on the occasion of the marriage of Louise Elizabeth, daughter of Louis XV, to the Infanto Dom Philippe, Grand Admiral of Spain, which took place in Paris on 29th, 30th and 31st August 1739. The present plate was drawn and engraved by Jacques François Blondel who had himself published, only the year before, his *De la Distribution des Maisons de Plaisance et de la Décoration des Edifices en General*, a work that was widely read and was one of the chief expressions of French high rococo taste. Here we see a detail from a section through the Hôtel de Ville in Paris, during a splendid ball held on 30th August. The courtyard (right, in this illustration) was covered over and turned into a ballroom on to which the windows of the rooms on the main floor opened. Details of the superb decorations, many specially contrived for the occasion, are clearly shown. In the book are also illustrations of the elaborate illuminations set up on and along the quays of the Seine on 29th August. All this is minutely described. The cost of these festivities must have been prodigious. The work is bound in red morocco with gold tooling, the royal fleur-de-lys at each corner and the coat of arms of the City of Paris in the centre. **Architectural Library, 26   Engraving (complete): 430mm × 800mm**

# THE MODEL ROOM

**Fig. 122**   This especially fine wooden model is a 'client model' sent to the banker William Mackworth Praed who had engaged Soane to build for him a house at Tyringham in Buckinghamshire. The roof and each of the upper floors can be lifted off to show the internal structure. The model was executed in 1793–4 by Joseph Parkins from drawings supplied by Soane and is one of three models connected with Tyringham which survive – the other two are for the bridge and the gateway and lodges. This model was given to the Museum in 1918 by Mr. F.A. Konig who was then the owner of the house. It is the only 'client' model in the collection. Later in the 19th century a dome was added to Tyringham House which is now a health clinic. Soane also built Praed's Bank in Fleet Street for the same client in 1801; the building was demolished in 1923. Soane recalled in his *Memoirs* that

the building of Tyringham House 'engaged a large portion of six of the most happy years of my life'.

Soane's collection of architectural models is of great importance. It contains over one hundred models of his own works – mostly produced in order to show clients what he was proposing, or to explain points of construction to builders and others. Soane used models more extensively than any other architect between the 1780s and 1830s, following a long-established practice going back to Wren and Hawksmoor – and, indeed, back into the Middle Ages. He insisted in his lectures that, in his own experience, 'whenever the model has been dispensed with, I am afraid the building has suffered in consequence thereof, either in solidity or convenience, and perhaps both'.

**Museum number: X236**    30.5cm × 53.3cm × 48.2cm

**Fig. 123**    Highly finished plaster-of-Paris model of the Temple of Rome and Augustus at Pola in Istria, Yugoslavia. This model was among twenty models of 'restorations' of ancient Greek and Roman buildings made by the French modelmaker François Fouquet and purchased by Soane from Edward Cresy in May 1834 for £100. François Fouquet, along with his father, Jean Pierre, was an artist modelmaker working for architects and collectors in Paris from the 1790s until the 1830s. Jean Pierre made a model of the Capitol of Virginia for Thomas Jefferson, models for the École Polytechnique in Paris and also worked for Louis François Cassas, an artist-historiographer and collector. Cassas travelled widely before settling down in Paris and building up a large collection of architectural models, many based on his own drawings, made in cork or plaster by Fouquet. In 1806 Cassas opened his Gallery in the rue de Seine, containing seventy-six models of celebrated antique buildings with the intention of presenting a comprehensive view of architectural history to instruct students. He commissioned J.G. Legrand to publish a list of his exhibits as a guide for visitors. It is not known whether Soane saw Cassas's collection during his trip to Paris in August 1814, or where it was at that date (it had been sold to the state in 1813). However, there is a copy of Legrand's catalogue in his Library and his own choice of models in cork and plaster is very similar to the collection assembled by Cassas.

François Fouquet worked with his father making the same sort of models although his seem to be slightly smaller in scale. The Fouquets were well known to architect-collectors in England and both John Nash and Robert Smirke, as well as Soane, owned examples of their work. Cassas's work seems to have influenced François Fouquet as much as it did his father, although there is no proof that he made models for Cassas's collection. However, a number of his models in Soane's collection are clearly made directly from Cassas's theoretical reconstructions published in *Voyage pittoresque de la Syrie, de la Phoenicie, de la Palestine et de la Basse Egypt* (1798–9), a copy of which Soane owned. Others, however, are fairly exact representations of celebrated Roman or Greek buildings still standing during Fouquet's lifetime. This model falls into the

latter category. The temple at Pola was one of a pair flanking a much larger temple on the north side of the forum, and was built between 2 AD and 14 AD. It had always been regarded as a key Roman building and was much favoured by Renaissance architects in particular. Andrea Palladio surveyed it and included his theoretical reconstructions in the *Quattro Libri*, of which Soane owned no less than four copies. Palladio's drawings suggest that there were sculptures on the roofline and in front of the portico. Cassas also drew the Temple, both in its late 18th-century dilapidated state and theoretically reconstructed. His drawings were published by Joseph Levallée in his *Voyage pittoresque de l'Istrie et Dalmatie* (1802), a copy of which is also in Soane's Library. However, for this model Fouquet did not precisely follow Cassas's theoretical drawings, which show a more elaborate doorcase and decorative angels and embellishments at either end of the inscriptions; he preferred a less fanciful approach based on the building as it stood during his lifetime.

**Museum number: MR26    14.2cm × 9.7cm**

# THE FAÇADE

**Fig. 124**   A design perspective by one of Soane's pupils for the façade of No. 13 Lincoln's Inn Fields, made late in August 1812. This design is as executed. It will be seen that the openings of the projecting 'loggia', as Soane called it, were not glazed originally; the windows were set back in line with the common street frontage on the north side of the square, leaving the projecting 'verandah' or loggia open. In 1825 the four 14th-century stone corbels from the north front of Westminster Hall were set into the façade and the top storey was added. In 1834 the windows were moved out to fill the loggia openings which made the 'verandah' part of the internal space, as it is today.

Throughout July and early August 1812 Soane had been experimenting with other ideas for the treatment of the upper parts of the loggia and there are eight other drawings in the collection showing some of these notions – one with a large domed finial over the central feature and another with four caryatid figures. The present top storey forming the third floor, added later by Soane, rather unbalanced the amazing design which some people at the time found 'a palpable eyesore', but which has enjoyed in the present century widespread admiration for its clean lines, its smooth and finely cut finish, and controlled elegance. Many people today see a resemblance between Soane's creation and Modernistic architecture of the 1920s and '30s, to the extent that it is sometimes supposed that the loggia is a later addition to Soane's Museum.

**Drawing 14.6.2    780mm × 450mm**

**Fig. 125**    Schematic model in wood for the loggia on the front of No. 13 Lincoln's Inn Fields, the home of Mr. and Mrs. John Soane, made in 1812 when Soane was preparing to rebuild the property to create the house now to be seen on this site. In July 1812 Soane noted that he was at work on plans of the 'next house' (at that time he lived next door at No. 12) and on 17th July the demolition of the existing house on the No. 13 site began. However, there was then trouble with the District Surveyor, Mr. Kinnard, who took Soane to court over the projecting 'loggia' or open verandah being built on the front of his new house, which extended 3ft 6in beyond the fronts of the adjoining houses, alleging a contravention of the Building Act. Soane argued that his loggia did not deprive neighbouring properties of light or air and was not a public nuisance or impediment since it was within the bounds of his freehold property. The case was widely reported and the newspaper cuttings kept by Soane are still in the Archive. *The Sun* newspaper of 15th October 1812 reported that during the case Soane's lawyer had 'stated that, so far from Mr. Soane's building (of which he exhibited a model) being an injury, it was an ornament to the square, and he produced models of two other buildings, namely Mr. Pearce's, and Surgeon's Hall, of far greater projection, the one which had received the sanction of the Magistrates upon a similar information having been laid, and the other had never been complained of at all'. It seems certain that this little model is the one presented in court because it is shown in a sketch of the Upper Drawing Office at 13 Lincoln's Inn Fields, dated 1812 (PSA15) flanked by two other models on the same small scale which clearly show the projecting portico of the College of Surgeons (built by Soane's master, George Dance) and the semi-circular first floor bay, supported on columns, of No. 51 Lincoln's Inn Fields, at that time occupied by a Mr. Pearce. Unfortunately neither of these other two models survive in the Museum (nor do the projections concerned – they are only recorded in drawings and photographs). The case was heard on 12th October 1812 at Bow Street and the magistrates declared in Soane's favour. Kinnard's subsequent application to the Court of King's Bench for a writ against Soane was also turned down on 18th November 1812. In December Soane received a congratulatory letter from his friend Rowland Burdon (see Fig. 85) saying, 'you have defended Yourself and castle strenuously and successfully. You have, in martial language, "Covered yourself with Glory"' and enclosing a cheque towards Soane's legal costs. No. 13 was finally ready for occupation in October 1813. Soane later incorporated the loggia into the rooms behind on all three floors. By the time he made this alteration William Kinnard, the District Surveyor in 1812, was no longer in office and his successor did not complain about Soane's action, which extended the internal space of three floors on No. 13 by 3½ feet beyond the accepted building line on the north side of the fields.

**Museum number: M1242    24.7cm × 18.4cm**

**Fig. 126** The pair of caryatids on the balcony of the projecting second floor 'loggia' on the front of No. 13 Lincoln's Inn fields are of Coade Stone. Soane paid £41 to Coade & Seeley at Lambeth for them in November 1812, the year that he rebuilt No. 13. At present they are coated with many layers of paint but they would have looked more like natural stone when new. One of the pleasures enjoyed by the Curator of Sir John Soane's Museum is to have these two ladies standing just outside his office window, looking out across the square. Soane pointed out in his 1830 *Description* that 'these statues are nearly opposite those of Machaon and Podalirius in the front of the College of Surgeons on the South side of the Square', – a building designed by Soane's master and friend, George Dance. The figures are based on the famous caryatids which support the roof of the south porch of the Erechtheion (see Fig. 71). Soane used similar figures on the second floor of the staircase hall at Buckingham House, Pall Mall in 1796 (now demolished), at Pitzhanger (see Fig. 41) and in the dome of the Rotunda at the Bank of England. The Erechtheion is visible in the background of James Ward's portrait of Fanny (Fig. 97). In the Museum Library is an original catalogue of the statues and ornaments available in Coade Stone (see also Fig. 72). This illustration shows some of the caryatids which are illustrated in the Coade catalogue. The Soane Museum's particular version of the caryatid is lacking, perhaps because it was a special model or possibly because Soane removed the page from the catalogue when placing his order and it therefore presumably no longer survives. **Architectural Library, SC.1.   233mm × 299mm**

# SOANE AS A COLLECTOR

## HELEN DOREY

Sir John Soane's collection was put together in England, rather than shipped back from a Grand Tour, as were many others, and he acquired items from a great many different sources.

Chief amongst these were the various sale-rooms, both in London and the provinces. Several hundred sale catalogues survive at the Museum, from at least twenty different auction-houses, and show that Soane must have haunted the salerooms. Many catalogues were sent to him by auctioneers like James Christie or by friends like the antiquary and topographer John Britton and the sculptor Richard Westmacott. They are often annotated to bring particular items to his notice. If Soane regarded any sale as especially important he obtained several copies of the catalogue; for example, he had five for the 1818 Robert Adam sale. Naturally, he often went to view collections even if he did not buy. He even bought some historic sale catalogues, including several of royal collections and the catalogue of the sale of Christopher Wren's sons' effects, held in 1749.

Soane did not always bid in person but regularly employed agents. Until her death, Mrs. Soane was among them, bidding for Hogarth's *Rake's Progress* at Christie's in 1802. She also purchased two Turner watercolours directly from Turner's Gallery in 1804. John Britton frequently sought out books for Soane's library. In addition Soane often commissioned his cabinet-maker John Robbins, his painter and glazier William Watson and a Mr Walker to act for him. One important piece was acquired on 6th March 1823 when Priestley and Weale (a well-known firm of booksellers) bid on behalf of Soane for a pilaster capital from the Pantheon (Fig. 84), as well as a fine Greek vase, at Christie's. In 1825 James Adams of Portsmouth, an ex-pupil of Soane's, was commissioned to bid at the North sale in nearby Alverstoke. He sent Soane detailed descriptions of the objects available, which were accompanied by meticulous watercolours. In his letters Adams points out that bargains cannot be expected at the sale because Mr. Christie is coming down from London to conduct it in person! However, in the end about a dozen items were bought.

Once purchased, goods might be collected by cart (sometimes by Soane's pupils), or conveyed to Lincoln's Inn Fields by a porter employed by the auction house. To admit the Belzoni sarcophagus and the cast of the Apollo Belvedere into the building, large holes had to be made in the back wall onto Whetstone Park. One can still see where these were filled in. Occasionally goods were returned to the auctioneers, presumably because no suitable place could be found for them in Soane's display. After the Bessborough sale in 1801 Soane retained eleven lots, for which he had paid £210, and returned four lots worth £97.

Soane sometimes bought directly from other collectors or from their heirs. Both the Dance and Adam collections of drawings were purchased from the architects' families. Private negotiations also led to the purchase of the Egyptian sarcophagus in 1824 after its refusal by the British Museum.

An enormous number of gifts were made to Soane for his museum. A Charles Percier drawing (Fig. 120) was a birthday present from Maria Denman, while a number of sculptures by Thomas Banks were presented to Soane in 1834 by his daughter, Mrs. Lavinia Forster. Colleagues and friends fell over themselves to present copies of their own publications to

Soane's library or to execute commissions for him, even before the 1833 Act of Parliament establishing the Museum as a permanent institution. C.H. Tatham gave his drawings of the Holland-Tatham marbles 'with the feeling only of gratification that they might be found in a corner of your invaluable Museum', while Henry Howard referred to his ceiling paintings in the Library and Dining-Room as 'my monument'. A few who offered their entire collections to Soane were, however, turned down. In 1821 Soane was offered the cast collection of John Sanders, his first pupil, on condition that Sanders received 'full credit . . . for having collected them and presented them to the public'. Although Soane later claimed he had rejected the casts on grounds of lack of space it seems more likely that he was not prepared to give Sanders the prominent credit which he demanded. During the clearing up of Sanders' estate in Reigate, Soane seems to have acquired his collection of cork models of the great temples at Paestum, for which, being dead, Sanders could no longer claim credit. John Sainsbury, who spent fifteen years gathering Napoleon memorabilia, offered his collection to Soane in 1835 and was also turned down, perhaps genuinely because of space problems, although a catalogue of his collection is in Soane's Library.

Soane sometimes purchased items out of charity. A letter of 1825 from John Taylor, editor of *The Sun*, recalls, 'about thirty years ago I met you at Christies during the sale of the effects of a Mr. Playfair [James Playfair, the Scottish architect], where I well remember that you bought many articles for the sake of the widow, none of which you wanted. This circumstance struck me at the time and has never been effaced from my memory.' Soane's commission of a painting of a scene from *The Merchant of Venice* from Francis Danby in 1828 was also an act of charity, cooked up with the help of Sir Francis Chantrey, the sculptor. Danby was paid £100 for the picture and Chantrey recorded that this had been the means of 'keeping him from sinking'.

One item, the so-called 'Napoleon pistol', said to have been presented by the Csar of Russia to Napoleon at Tilsit in 1807, and obtained in 1826, from Alexander Dry, a pawnbroker in St. Martin's Lane, was purchased after Soane read of its existence in the newspapers.

Building sites were a fruitful source of objects for Soane's museum and he took every opportunity to collect items or to take casts. As a result, his collection contains probably the only surviving parts of the celebrated Painted Chamber at Westminster (Fig. 50). He also salvaged furniture from Yarborough House (formerly Walpole House) in Chelsea, which he demolished to make way for the Chelsea Hospital Infirmary. The gleanings included the splendid 'Walpole Desk', now in the New Picture Room. Medieval arches were brought from Westminster and used to create the mock abbey ruins in the Monk's Yard. Soane also acquired several decorative elements from Carlton House, a building he particularly admired, when it was demolished in 1827. He carefully preserved capitals from Sir Robert Taylor's Bank of England (which he demolished) and obtained term figures from Furnival's Inn, a 17th-century building on Holborn, when it was demolished.

Soane was a fellow of the Society of Antiquaries and was obviously interested in early archaeological discoveries. He may even have been involved in early excavations. We know that Mrs. Soane visited 'excavations' at Chertsey Abbey, and fragments of glass and pavement from that site are in her husband's collection. There are also several earthenware vessels (see Fig. 22) found during the excavation of foundations at various sites, including the Board of Trade in Whitehall and the new London Bridge. Their discovery was recorded meticulously by Soane, who indicated at what depth each piece was found. He even created an antiquarian interior in the form of the Monk's Parlour, for which he purchased numerous objects; instruments of torture, triptychs, candlesticks and stained glass, as well as having casts specially taken from carvings in Westminster Abbey by Thomas Palmer and Sons, to adorn the walls (see Fig. 49).

Soane acquired items for many different reasons. Some, like the Coade-Stone caryatids, the Apollo and the Belzoni sarcophagus were bought or accepted with particular positions in the Museum in mind. A few, like the sarcophagus and the Ephesian Diana, were extremely valuable and rare, while other items were purchased in groups largely for effect. Soane's collection of Antique Greek and Roman vases is a good example. He was primarily interested in vases for their refined shape and the overall impression created by groupings of them high up, rather than for their individual importance. Most of his forty or fifty vases were acquired as a job lot for £40 from the James Clerk sale at Christie's in 1802, and were eventually arranged on top of the Library bookcases at Lincoln's Inn Fields, where they were merely described as 'several Etruscan vases, rich in form and decoration' in Soane's 1835 *Description*. He had no qualms about including specimens of Wedgwood's imitation 'Etruscan' vases in the arrangements alongside the antique ones. Soane did, however, acquire two significant vases; the Cawdor vase for which he paid £65.5s. at the sale of Lord Cawdor's effects and the Englefield vase, secured in 1823 for £24.13s.6d. Soane was attracted to both by their unusual features; the Cawdor was exceptionally large while the Englefield was of 'extraordinary design and preservation'. When he moved into Lincoln's Inn Fields he used the Cawdor vase, perched on top of a pile of fragments in the basement beneath the Dome, as a centrepiece for his Museum; it was later replaced by the sarcophagus.

In all aspects of his collecting Soane often seems to have been attracted by bizarre or curious items. These included some that had also been selected by the Abbé Montfaucon for illustration in his *L'Antiquité Expliquée* (1719), which gave them extra prestige. The Ephesian Diana is one such. Soane was similarly attracted to a bronze lamp at the Yarnold sale (see Fig. 3), probably because it had been included in Montfaucon. He also collected a great number of 'natural curiosities' including shark and elephant teeth, a Neptune's Cup Sponge, strangely shaped bits of wood and fossils. These were items often included in the popular 'shows' of his day, such as that of William Bullock at the Egyptian Hall in Piccadilly, which we know he visited.

A wide variety of objects in the collection were bought because they served as reminders of famous people and events, both historical and contemporary. These ranged from the death-mask of Parker the Mutineer (Richard Parker c. 1767–97), 'remarkable for its similarity to that of Oliver Cromwell' to the Naseby Jewel, purchased for Soane at a sale in Bristol by Maria Denman and said to have been dropped by King Charles I while fleeing the battlefield of Naseby. Soane also acquired an ivory table and chairs, captured at Seringapatam in southern India, at the defeat of Tippoo Sultan in 1799. These 'costly and delicate memorials' served a moral purpose. Soane wrote that they 'remind us of his [Tippoo's] vices and bid us rejoice in his fall'. The existence of the celebrated East India Company Museum, which displayed a great many items looted from Seringapatam, perhaps encouraged him to acquire them. The astronomical clock (Fig. 5), as well as having a superb and unusual movement, may have attracted Soane because of its royal provenance. A more dubious acquisition was a very modest 17th-century tortoiseshell casket, said to have been a gift from Philip II of Spain to Mary Tudor. A number of books in the collection were probably acquired purely because of their distinguished provenance; indeed many were duplicates. Among these were William Beckford's copy of Gray's *Poems* and William Hamilton's own copy of his *Antiquities* as well as 'the most extraordinary copy in the world' of Visconti's *Museo Pio Clementino*, described thus because it had belonged to Pope Pius VI (Pope 1775–99). Soane added the manuscript *Catalogus Plantarum*, a list of plants in the botanic gardens at Padua, by J.A. Bonato, to his already extensive Napoleonic collection in 1823, purely because it had been in the Empress Joséphine's library at Malmaison.

Soane was a great admirer of Napoleon, in common with Henry Holland and many other contemporaries. Even after the Emperor's final defeat and exile his fascination did not diminish. Soane acquired portraits, busts, the pistol and a gold ring containing a lock of Napoleon's hair, as well as a number of books, some from the Imperial library. On his trips to Paris in 1814 and 1819 Soane was particularly on the lookout for items with a Napoleonic connection, returning from the second visit with the Empress's own magnificent copy of Percier and Fontaine's *Palais et Maisons de Rome* (Fig. 11) and a copy of their *Descriptions des Cérémonies . . . pour le marriage de S M L'Empereur Napoleon avec . . . Marie-Louise d'Autriche*, as well as a volume about the *Campagnes de Buonaparte*. One of the two portraits of Napoleon, which Soane displayed flanking the Emperor's pistol in the Breakfast Room was at first only lent to him by Lady Beechey, who at the time commented on 'the high estimation in which you hold the great talents of Bonaparte'. It was later presented to Soane by Sir William Beechey as a token of regard. This is the only example of a loan to the Museum during Soane's lifetime. A sword said to have been presented to Napoleon by one of his officers is also in Soane's collection; it is of the right date and so could be what it is claimed to be. A less certain claim is that Soane's collection of 140 Napoleon medals (Figs. 109/110) actually belonged to the Empress Joséphine.

Egyptian antiquities fascinated Soane, again in common with many contemporaries. They were spellbound by the awe-inspiring antiquity of treasures like the sarcophagus of Seti I and fascinated by the mystery of its indecipherable hieroglyphics. Soane was equally intrigued by the romance of Belzoni, an Italian strong-man turned archaeologist and the discoverer of the sarcophagus in the tomb of Seti I. He always referred to his greatest treasure as the 'Belzoni sarcophagus' and bemoaned in a lecture that he had not been able to avail himself as he would have wished 'of the labours of [this] enterprising and zealous traveller'. He was therefore particularly keen to acquire items from Belzoni's collections when they appeared in the Yarnold sale in 1825 and snapped up the 'Belzoni jug' (fragments of a bronze vessel found at the Oasis of Aamon) from Belzoni's sale in 1822. Among the other Egyptian items Soane purchased were *stelae*, a mummy case, a mummy's head and many small *ushabti* figures and bronzes for display on tables throughout the house, sometimes in glass cases.

As befitted one who delighted in creating theatrical effects, Soane's collection is full of theatrical memorabilia, particularly items related to the works of Shakespeare. He was a frequent theatre-goer, familiar with the celebrated performances of Charles Kean, Sarah Siddons and her brother John Phillip Kemble, and his collection contains a life-mask of Mrs Siddons and busts of Kemble by both John Gibson and Flaxman as well as a portrait of Kemble as Coriolanus by Sir Francis Bourgeois. Soane attended the dinner given to mark Kemble's farewell to the stage in 1817 and acquired from Flaxman casts of the silver reliefs showing 'Kemble crowned by Melpomene' and 'Kemble inspired by the Genius of Shakespeare' which were on the vase presented to the actor on that occasion. Soane also owned a copy of the Kemble sale catalogue of 1821, in which every buyer and price is written in neatly, although he did not purchase anything himself. As well as Kemble memorabilia Soane also bought a number of theatrical prints and a bust of Richard Brinsley Sheridan by George Garrard. The Flaxman chessmen (Fig. 88) also have a theatrical association, the King and Queen being modelled on Kemble and Siddons as Macbeth and his wife.

Literature was always a special interest of Soane's, and just as he sought to pay tribute to British artists, so he wished to pay tribute to the great figures of English literature in his collection. Supreme among these was, of course, Shakespeare, in whose honour the Shakespeare Recess was created in 1829 (see Fig. 99). This was perhaps inspired by earlier structures devoted to the Bard, such as the Rotunda at David Garrick's villa at Hampton. A number of busts of Shakespeare, as well as John Hamilton Mortimer's etchings of Shakespearian characters, are in the Museum. Towards the end of his life Soane increasingly commissioned paintings for his Museum, choosing the subjects himself. These commissions are dominated by Shakespearian themes. Soane's enthusiasm was probably inspired by Alderman John Boydell's 'Shakespeare Gallery' in Pall Mall, which opened in 1789 and finally closed in 1805. Boydell commissioned 167 large-scale paintings of Shakespearian themes, with the object of establishing 'an English School of historical painting' and producing prints for widespread sale. He hoped, like Soane, to leave his Gallery to the nation, thus establishing a national memorial to Shakespeare, but financial difficulties prevented this. Mrs. Soane bought two paintings from the sale of the contents of the Gallery, including the large oil painting by Durno of 'Falstaff in diguise led out by Mrs. Page', which cost a mere nine guineas. Henry Howard's 'Vision of Shakespeare' (1830) was commissioned especially for the Shakespeare Recess, and Soane also acquired two other oils by the same artist: 'The Contention of Oberon and Titania' and 'Lear and Cordelia'. In the Picture Room Recess hangs a watercolour, commissioned from Soane's close friend Clara Maria Pope, entitled 'The Bust of Shakespeare Encircled by All the Flowers Mentioned in his Works'. This once-charming piece shows the flowers garlanding Soane's plaster bust of Shakespeare, after Rysbrack, which stands in a niche on the staircase. The picture is now sadly faded or it would have been included in the present selection.

Soane's love for Shakespeare went hand-in-hand with enormous admiration for the poems of John Milton, who had extolled the bard in *On Shakespeare* and *L'Allegro*. The latter poem described Shakespeare as 'fancy's child' and was the inspiration for the subject of Howard's 'Vision of Shakespeare', which was chosen by Soane. The picture shows Shakespeare 'seated in the lap of fancy'. Milton's *Comus* may have inspired the commissioning of another of Howard's works, 'Circe', in the early 1830s. Moreover, Howard's paintings in the Library-Dining Room are described by Soane using words from *Paradise Lost* in the 1835 *Description*. Soane also owned Richard Westall's painting 'Milton Composing Paradise Lost' (1802). Paintings illustrating artistic genius at work were obviously very much to his taste. In 1825 he asked C. L. Eastlake to execute a painting for his Museum based on verses from Edmund Spenser's *Faerie Queen*, the subject being 'Una Delivering the Red Cross Knight from the Cave of Despair'. In his own copy of Spenser's works Soane marked the section in the Introduction which described the discovery of Spenser's genius, as well as the verses he asked Eastlake to illustrate, the very ones which had caught the eye of Sir Philip Sidney when Spenser sent them to him.

Soane sought out for his library not just first editions of the works of Shakespeare and Milton but copies which had belonged to the actors Kemble and Garrick. When John Britton purchased Kemble's first folio Shakespeare (1623) on Soane's behalf at the James Boswell sale he wrote that he had 'bag'd the prize' for Soane's 'larder' where 'it will long keep, be always in good flavour, and do honour to the possessor – it will afford a perpetually standing dish on the table of genius and talent – never create surfeit but "increase appetite" by its almost miraculous qualities'. Other

precious literary editions in Soane's library included two 16th-century Italian copies of Boccaccio's *Decameron*, as well as numerous works by the great authors of antiquity.

Above all else Soane built up a huge collection of items related to architecture. His casts of antique ornament and architectural elements were constantly studied by his pupils and his Academy students. Indeed, his pupils spent days painstakingly making watercolour copies of fragments from the collection as part of their training. Soane himself could use the collection for reference in his own work and it was also a reminder of the happy years he had spent in Italy as a young man. He was naturally particularly keen to acquire collections built up by practising architects during the 18th century, beginning with casts brought from Italy by James Playfair, purchased in 1795. At the sale of 'The Athenian Reveley' (the architect Willey Reveley) in 1801, Soane bought the entire collection of casts, between forty and fifty items. These, too, had been brought back from Italy and included casts from most of the major Roman buildings and the Museo Clementinum (later the Pio-Clementino). Later, with increased space at 13 Lincoln's Inn Fields, Soane went on to acquire Henry Holland's marbles in 1816 and to make extensive purchases at the Adam sale. His last large-scale acquisition of casts after the antique was from Lewis Wyatt, an Office of Works colleague, in 1834. These casts had been made for Wyatt in Rome in 1820 by Benedetto, an assistant of the celebrated sculptor Canova – a fact that may have made them seem particularly attractive to Soane. Wyatt was forced to sell his collection when he lost his post in 1832 and had to remove his casts from Hampton Court, where he had stored them for a while. He sold ninety-one casts with a MSS catalogue to Soane for £52.10s. Among the pieces was the Stork and Serpent from the Vatican Museum visible in Fig. 59. The collection also included casts from statues in the famous Roman collection of the Polish Prince Stanislas Poniatowsky, set up in the 1790s, which Soane must have known by repute, as well as from the Temple of Vesta at Tivoli, the Temples of Jupiter Stator and Antonius Faustina, Trajan's Forum, the Sistine Chapel, the Villa Borghese, the Vatican Museums, the Villa Albani, the Church of S. Maria del Popolo and Trajan's Column – all of which Soane knew well.

Soane's cast collections included not just architectural items but casts of antique sculpture. Soane believed strongly that in order to achieve 'perfection in architecture' it was necessary to study sculpture and painting as well. His mentor, Sir William Chambers, had sent him off to Italy with a copy of a letter, urging him to 'study painting and sculpture thoroughly, [for] you cannot be a master in your own art without great judgement in these, which are so intimately connected with it'. Of all the famous antique statues Soane seems to have singled out three or four for particular attention. He prized his large cast of the Apollo Belvedere, placed symbolically at the centre of the Museum, and later added to his collection a large plaster of the head alone and another smaller plaster model of the whole statue, by Flaxman. He also owned no less than four versions of the Farnese Hercules and three of the Venus de Medici.

As well as collections of casts and marbles Soane 'never lost any opportunity of collecting every Book and print that came within reach on the subject of architecture' for the benefit of his pupils and students. When he left Italy in 1780 it was 'with heart-felt sorrow in firm hopes of seeing it again', and although he never did, he amassed a remarkable collection of guide-books and other publications about its monuments. Some were purchased because he had met the authors and many because they reminded him of places he had seen. Labruzzi's publication on the Appian Way (Fig. 61) and Hamilton's *Campi Phlegraei* (Fig. 10) combined both these attractions. His numerous books about the remains of antiquity also included special treasures, such as a proof copy of Thomas Major's *Paestum* and copies of the publications of Piranesi, Robert Adam and Stuart and Revett. Soane particularly treasured the items connected with

Giovanni Baptista Piranesi, the great perspectivist, in whose etchings of reconstructions of Roman buildings lay the roots of neoclassicism. Amongst his antiquities were a number which had come via Piranesi's workshop or had been engraved by him, and his collection of architectural drawings included Piranesi's fifteen views of the great Temples at Paestum (Fig. 34). Soane also greatly valued the works of Charles Louis Clérisseau, the French architect who had exerted so much influence on Robert Adam. Soane's collection of architectural drawings numbers 30,000 and has always been celebrated. He was inspired by the example of the great collections built up from the Renaissance onwards, by the artist Vasari (some of whose drawings he thought he owned, see Fig. 112), and by celebrated architect-collectors such as Inigo Jones, William and John Talman, Lord Burlington, and Robert Adam. Soane acquired items from their collections whenever possible as well as buying the drawings of 'modern' architects; Henry Holland, Sir William Chambers, George Dance and James Wyatt among others.

Soane also looked out for objects connnected with famous architects. He owned Sir Christopher Wren's watch (Figs. 89/90) and what he thought was Wren's hollow malacca walking-stick containing compass, dividers, ivory scale, pen and five-foot rule, which he displayed prominently on the chimney-piece in his Study (in fact it dates from about 1800!). A wooden model of four classical Orders was acquired because it, too, was said to have belonged to Wren. Soane once owned a set of drawing instruments which had belonged to Stuart and Revett, although these are no longer in the collection. He also displayed in his Museum busts of Sir William Chambers, George Dance, Palladio, Wren and Inigo Jones. In addition he owned autograph letters by Wren and Jones. He had a personal reason for valuing the work of Jones particularly highly, having won the RA silver medal in 1772 with drawings of Jones' Banqueting House in Whitehall. He was later entrusted with its restoration in 1829, re-designing the roof structure and salvaging a pilaster capital from the façade for his Museum.

Among the architectural collection on display in the Museum, Soane included many of his own drawings and models. They were intended to form part of the collection which he left to posterity and were deliberately displayed in association with the celebrated buildings of antiquity. His Upper Drawing Office is in the midst of the Museum, not even separated from it by solid walls, while his original arrangement in the Picture Room had a wall of Gandy's portrayals of his own works facing his Piranesi drawings of the Temples of Paestum. There can be no doubt but that these juxtapositions were intentional.

The influence of the Royal Academy on Soane's collecting was profound. His long association with the Academy began at the age of eighteen, and throughout his life he devoted a considerable amount of time each year to preparing his own drawings for inclusion in the annual exhibition. His collections of paintings and sculpture are largely composed of the works of fellow Academicians. Prime amongst these were founder members of the Academy: Sir Joshua Reynolds, its first President; Sir William Chambers, its first Treasurer and George Dance, Soane's 'revered master'. Soane owned items by all three. Reynolds had presented him with the Academy's gold medal in 1776 and an account of the ceremony records that his speech in praise of the young architect was exceptionally fulsome. This may possibly explain why examples of Reynolds' work are in the collection while the work of other celebrated contemporaries like Constable and Gainsborough is unrepresented. Sir William Chambers was also held in particular esteem by Soane; he had been responsible for introducing the young architect to George III and therefore indirectly securing for him the trip to Italy which was to have such a profound influence on his work.

Other Royal Academy contacts whose work is included in Soane's collection were J.C.F. Rossi, a talented sculptor who won the gold medal

in 1784; Christopher Hunneman, who painted a portrait of Soane (always said to have been done in Rome, but possibly painted in 1776 when both were studying at the Academy), and Nathaniel Marchant, a set of whose '100 Impressions from Gems' (sulphur casts) hangs in the Dressing Room. Soane also probably first met J.M.W. Turner, Sir Thomas Lawrence and the sculptors Sir Francis Chantrey and Thomas Banks through the Royal Academy.

Of all Soane's Academy contacts, however, the sculptor John Flaxman, who became a close personal friend, was the most important. Amongst Soane's earliest purchases, in the spring of 1790, were two lions and a pair of vases from Flaxman, which were prominently displayed in the Breakfast Room at No. 12, Lincoln's Inn Fields. During his lifetime Flaxman gave Soane a number of items, including a pair of plaster profile portraits of himself and his wife which hang on the Staircase. The majority of the Flaxman sculptures in Soane's collection, however, were acquired in the decade after the sculptor's death in 1826, from another great friend, Maria Denman, Flaxman's sister-in-law. Soane seems to have approached her at various dates seeking appropriate pieces from amongst the works of his old friend for special positions in his Museum. On one occasion, in June 1833, Miss Denman offered to 'walk through your museum in order to ascertain what places there are to receive works of art – as to dimension and form – as by that I think your choice must be regulated'. From Miss Denman came not only Flaxman's own sculptures, but his studio skeleton (Fig. 54) and pieces of antique sculpture, including the large panel of Perseus and Andromeda visible in Fig. 59.

Apart from the works of Flaxman, the rest of Soane's sculpture collection consisted mainly of works purchased from Royal Academy colleagues and friends, with the intention of promoting British artists. Indeed, many of the sculptures are portraits of friends; busts of Chambers and Dance, two of Sir Thomas Lawrence and even one of John Baily, one of Soane's plasterers. In addition there are a number of busts and statues, often by Academy colleagues, of people Soane admired: Cuvier (Fig. 44), Blücher (Fig. 46), the composer Handel, Ben Jonson, Reynolds, Camden, and Warren Hastings. There is also a large plaster model by Turnerelli, sculptor to the King, of George III, who had awarded Soane his travelling scholarship in 1778. Soane also collected a number of busts and statues of William Pitt. Very little is known about Soane's personal political allegiance but it is interesting that his great friend, John Taylor, observed in a letter of June 1822, 'I know that you set a value on whatever relates to Mr Pitt.'

All Soane's collections; sculpture, paintings and objects, testify to the fact that he was always conscious of the public role of his Museum as a record of the celebrated men and events of his own times.

In the Conclusion to his 1835 *Description* Soane wrote 'the best efforts in my power have been exerted, on every occasion, to promote the interest and advantage of British artists, by giving commissions to some of the living and by collecting together as many of the works of our highly talented deceased countrymen as I had the means to purchase, or suitable places wherein to deposit and exhibit them to advantage'. Oddly enough, in view of this, the first oil-painting Soane purchased, in 1800, was by an Italian, Zuccarelli, perhaps bought because it had belonged to the celebrated collector William Beckford. By and large it was during the early years of his collecting that Soane purchased the few foreign paintings and drawings which can now be seen on the walls at Lincoln's Inn Fields. These included works he thought were by Veronese and Rubens (see Fig. 100). He also purchased Watteau's '*Accordée du Village*' in 1802 and three Canalettos, the largest of which (Fig. 83) came from the 1807 sale of Beckford's collection at Fonthill Splendens. Although there were a great many collections of old masters coming onto the European market at the time when Soane was buying his pictures, he did not choose to buy from them, although he often collected the catalogues. Soane's picture collection contains no works by Claude, so popular with English 18th-century collectors, nor does it contain any of the Dutch genre also popular in England. Instead, it contains works like 'The Cheat Detected', an early example of English genre painting by Edward Bird, and the landscapes of Callcott (Fig. 36). Few of the contemporaries whose works Soane purchased are celebrated today. The names of Sir Francis Bourgeois, Henry Howard, William Hamilton and Maria Cosway, for example, are relatively unknown. Only J.M.W. Turner, Soane's great friend, and Henry Fuseli are generally well known. Fuseli, the most eccentric of all romantic artists, valued poetical (that is, historical or narrative) painting above realistic art (portraits, for example). Soane obviously agreed. He shared the feeling for 'the terrible sublime' evoked in the works of Fuseli, James Barry, John Martin and John Mortimer, all of whose work is represented in his collection though, in the case of the last three, only in the form of prints or drawings. His taste also ran to narrative subjects from history, such as William Hamilton's 'Richard II Landing at Milford Haven' and Hilton's 'Mark Anthony Reading Caesar's Will' (commissioned in 1834).

Soane bought few examples of British painting of earlier centuries, apart from works by Hogarth. In fact, he was at the forefront of a Hogarth revival in the early nineteenth century along with the Prince Regent, Alderman Boydell (of the Shakespeare Gallery) and John Julius Angerstein, who owned the *Marriage à la Mode* series (which was to pass with the rest of his collection to the National Gallery). Soane's Hogarth collection began with the purchase of a copy of Samuel Ireland's *Hogarth Illustrated*, published by Boydell between 1791 and 1798, and he went on to acquire the collection of proof engravings given by Hogarth to Dr. Isaac Schomberg at the Nicholas Revett sale in 1804. However, his greatest Hogarth treasures were his two series of paintings for which he paid extremely high prices. His determination to acquire the *Rake's Progress* series is shown by the fact that Mrs. Soane herself went to bid on his behalf when he was unable to attend. *An Election* was knocked down to Soane at the huge price of 1,650 guineas in 1823, the auctioneer reportedly announcing, 'As returning officer, I have the honour of declaring that John Soane Esq. is the successful candidate in this warmly contested Election.'

The quality of the star items in Soane's collection is undisputed. He paid high prices for a number of individual pieces and spent an enormous amount of time modifying his rooms to display them in the best possible way. However, he was often competing at the sale-rooms with men like Henry Blundell, collecting for his magnificent sculpture gallery at Ince Blundell near Liverpool; Thomas Hope, whose fine London house in Duchess Street, largely rebuilt just after 1800, was the subject of a well-illustrated monograph, and Charles Townley, most of whose antiquities are now in the British Museum. At the sales of great collections like those of the Earl of Bessborough and Lord Mendip in the early 1800s, these men bought the most expensive pieces while Soane made major purchases among the lower-priced items and thus acquired quantities of cinerary urns, altars and small statues. Occasionally Soane purchased items of doubtful integrity, almost certainly the work of notorious 18th-century Roman restorers like Bartolomeo Cavaceppi and Piranesi. Seven of the cinerary urns purchased from the Mendip sale have been described as 'dubious *pasticcios* of antique fragments or complete fabrications'. Among

these is one actually engraved by Piranesi in one of his 'trophies' of assorted fragments. At the Adam sale in 1818, too, Soane's extensive purchases included a series of heavily restored *vasi* which completed his striking display round the Dome (Fig. 55). Busts he bought from the sculptor Joseph Nollekens as antique are, in fact, antique draped lower parts with non-antique heads cleverly added. However, of approximately thirty antique bronzes, although some are probably forgeries, a few are extremely choice examples which it is believed must have come from Pompeii or Herculaneum. Soane also obtained some extremely good bargains. His large gem collection (Figs. 107/108) cost him only £1,000 in 1834 and was accompanied by a detailed list of all the gems, made by the Duke of Buckingham's Librarian.

Among Soane's sculptures are some pieces now known to be important but selected by Soane using simply his own judgement. He would have been delighted to know that he owned the only major piece of the Erechtheion frieze outside Greece (Fig. 71) which he knew only as a headless unidentified torso. A Roman bust he thought showed 'Augustus Caesar when a boy' has turned out to be an important member of a group of Roman copies of the so-called Westmacott Athlete type, after a Greek bronze by Polykleitos. Similarly, among Soane's Renaissance and 17th- and 18th-century sculpture, particularly the pieces bought from the Richard Cosway sale in 1821, are important works. Soane knew Cosway personally and was well aware of the high quality of his collection. Nevertheless, he did not know that the 'Figure of a Gentleman, in Terracotta' was Van Dyck by Rysbrack, nor that the 'Figure Resting on an Urn' would turn out to be the Guelfi model for the Craggs monument in Westminster Abbey (Fig. 18). Most important of all, he did not know that his terracotta of a seated woman was in fact the model for the figure of Architecture on Michaelangelo's tomb (Fig. 17). On the whole, despite the fact that he was sometimes taken in by forgeries, perhaps on account of their putatively distinguished provenances, he had an extremely good eye for quality.

Soane's collection, in all its variety, is a summary of his work and of his age, a record of the artistic life of England and the major political upheavals of his lifetime, as well as a collection for the student of architecture. It was also, for him, intensely personal, enshrining recollections of his friends and his beloved wife and transporting him, as he walked amongst it, back to Italy, the source of much of his creative inspiration. Isaac D'Israeli, an old friend of Soane's, recognised that the collection was for Soane a record of 'The Visions of the Morning and Dreams of the Evening of Life', the title Soane gave to one of Gandy's perspectives of his works. Mrs. Hofland, a friend of Soane's whose poetical descriptions of the house are interspersed with Soane's text in his 1835 *Description*, summed up the collection beautifully, finding that there were 'objects of deep interest alike to the antiquary, who loves to explore and retrace them through ages past; the student, who in cultivating a classic taste, becomes enamoured of their forms; and the imaginative man, whose excursive fancy gives to each "a local habitation and a name" in association with the most interesting events and the most noble personages the page of history has transmitted for our contemplation'.

# INDEX